THE FUTURE
OF WORK

Publisher's Note

The books in the *Forward Studies Series* contain a selection of research studies, reports, seminar or conference proceedings of the European Commission's Forward Studies Unit.

In publishing these works in the *Forward Studies Series*, the original material has undergone editorial rearrangement. Bibliographies have been added where necessary.

THE FUTURE OF WORK

Marjorie Jouen and Bénédicte Caremier

Preface by Patrick Venturini

Office for Official Publications of the European Communities

KOGAN PAGE

British Library Cataloguing in Publication Data
A CIP record for this book is available from the British Library

First published in 2000

© European Communities, 2000

Office for Official Publications of the European Communities
2 rue Mercier, L–2985 Luxembourg
ISBN 92-828-7860-0
Catalogue No CM-23-99-685-EN-C

Kogan Page
120 Pentonville Road, London N1 9JN
kpinfo@kogan-page.co.uk
www.kogan-page.co.uk

ISBN 0 7494 3427 9

Typeset by JS Typesetting, Wellingborough, Northants
Printed in Great Britain by Creative Print and Design, Wales

Contents

Acknowledgements

There is an invisible corps of people behind this publication. We are especially grateful to the Translation Department for their work. A special mention is owed to Jonathan Stockwell for his interest in the book, his enthusiasm and his rigour in correcting the English version.

Bénédicte Caremier
Marjorie Jouen

Preface

To lay the basis, at European level, for discussions on the future of work; to take a variety of approaches (economic, technological, sociological, etc.); to provide a forum in which the intellectual debate could emerge from its national cocoon and its technical bias to confront the multifarious and ever-changing aspects of the real situation; to take fuller account of national and regional sensitivities; and to evaluate the consequences of certain political choices for the Europe of the future: such were the aims of the deliberations which the European Commission's Forward Studies Unit and Directorate-General for Employment and Social Affairs embarked upon at the end of 1996.

This may have seemed an ambitious undertaking, as indeed it was. But the neutral, multidisciplinary approach taken enabled expectations to be met and a coherent framework to be set up for the huge task ahead. The launching of this European debate on the future of work was also intended as a contribution towards the discussions on modernization of the European social model, a subject on which all Community institutions have a duty to articulate their views.

The deliberations also revealed (if it was not already obvious) the full extent of the damage caused by unemployment over the past ten years. Employment is now the single most important issue for the European public, and has risen to the top of the political agenda too. In recent years, much welcome progress has been made in the fight to create jobs, thanks to prudent reforms, numerous individual or non-governmental initiatives, and improved policy co-ordination between governments. And yet, in our opinion, it would be a serious mistake to close the file on 'the future of work' because the vice-like grip of unemployment is slackening off.

Admittedly, the tide would seem to have turned. Dire predictions about the end of work and the information revolution are not taken so seriously as they once were. Those who have found work are feeling new confidence and their optimism is spreading to those around them. But modernization and restructuring have continued the process of economic globalization has picked up speed, and unemployment has left its mark. The services, which have replaced old manufacturing industries, call for different skills. New forms of exclusion have appeared, affecting specific groups and areas, and all kinds of inequalities, rather than fading away, are becoming more pronounced. The past ten years have seen far-reaching changes in the patterns of production and consumption.

As a structural phenomenon, unemployment has meant new roles to play for various economic, social and political protagonists. Although originally bound by cultural stereotypes and traditional practices, all of them (governments, the two sides of industry, institutions, associations, etc.) now seem to be setting off down a new path. They are now more careful in their reactions, more open to innovation and negotiation (or even co-operation) and more reluctant to engage in conflict.

It is precisely in this situation that the European institutions, and the Commission in particular, could perform a very useful function, not only by abandoning short-termism and taking a broad view of the issues facing a society which values the quest for prosperity above social cohesion and democracy, but also by making it easier to find and establish a new balance, by providing the framework for debate, by encouraging those involved to assume their responsibilities and by creating the conditions for progress.

The Economic and Social Committee, for its part, may prove to be a particularly useful partner in this venture, being the representative assembly and the forum for civil society at European level.

Europe's task is to encourage discussion (and even experimentation) concerning the changes that are taking place. The aim is not to construct a vision or a theoretical 'model', but to provide reference points in time (so we can better understand the current changes and assess the medium-term consequences of this or that choice) and in space (so we can find out about other people's practices and compare results). The experiences and aspirations of our contemporaries – men and women, young and old, in the cities and the countryside – may then give shape to a new development model in which work will occupy a different place.

Europe and all its component groups will thus have provided the impetus towards the modernization of society, in the best interests of the majority.

Patrick Venturini
Secretary-General of the Economic and Social Committee

Introduction

Since its inception, one of the goals of European integration has been to bring lasting peace to the continent through economic and social progress. This has been so successful that Europeans tend to take continued social cohesion and ever-improving living and working conditions for granted. Consequently – almost inevitably – the economic downturn at the beginning of the decade, after the completion of the internal market, dented people's faith in the European institutions; for more than ten years now, the unemployment rate and the measures taken to reduce it have been very reliable indicators of public support for European integration.

The Commission's first response in 1993 was to produce the White Paper on 'Growth, competitiveness and employment' and to explore different ways of combating unemployment. Then there was the 'Co-ordinated strategy for employment', in which the Member States were wholeheartedly involved, and the efforts to reinforce the social dimension of the Union in the new Treaty of Amsterdam.

However, while recognizing that unemployment in European countries is of a specific, structural kind – there has even been talk of a 'European disease' – the Commission could not, of course, ignore the world-wide phenomena affecting other developed economies. It had to look beyond employment as an isolated issue and examine in depth the changes in production methods and working conditions, the better to gauge the long-term consequences. In Western society, where work has, for centuries, supplied the framework for our social structures, these technological and economic changes have special repercussions. By undermining all the traditional functions of work – production,

1

redistribution and socialization – they reveal how the deepest aspirations and values of people in Europe are changing. Nor is it surprising that the growing debate on the end of work as we know it has quickly spread beyond a small group of specialists in the field to political circles, unions, professional associations and society at large.

To get a better idea of the complexity of the problem, before taking action or beginning research, the Commission organized two seminars on the future of work. The *Carrefours des sciences et de la culture* (European Seminars on Science and Culture) held in Leiden, the Netherlands, in October 1994, and in Lund, Sweden, a year later, brought together intellectuals from all the Member States (economists, sociologists, historians, anthropologists, geographers, political scientists and philosophers). On each occasion, Jacques Delors or Jacques Santer attended as President of the Commission to underline the importance they attached to the subject, and emphasize the wide-ranging nature of the debate. Jacques Delors said that the Leiden seminar was 'basically a reflection on the nature of work, not simply as a process of socialization, but as a process by which society reproduces itself'. At Lund, Jacques Santer pointed out that for many citizens today the European Union's (EU's) credibility and legitimacy are judged on its handling of unemployment, but that it would be wrong to pretend that fair, lasting solutions to a problem on this scale could be found without a broader debate on the role of employment in our societies now and in the future.

Though stimulating, the discussions tended to produce analyses and reveal avenues to be explored rather than actually delivering results of any direct use to political and economic leaders.

All the participants agreed that changes such as the development of 'atypical' forms of work, persistent unemployment in certain groups or areas, fragmented career profiles and the shifting dividing line between professional and private life, hastened by reform of the welfare state, had left Europeans and their political representatives in a state of confusion, and posed a threat to social cohesion. However, apart from general agreement that a return to full employment without social change was a pipe dream, recommendations differed substantially.

These discussions did, however, confirm the scale of the challenge facing the European Union and drew attention to the special role the Commission could play as a catalyst for thought. They served to underline the legitimacy of the Commission's action in the following respects:

- In terms of subsidiarity: Europe can complement the action taken by governments;
- In terms of the shared fate of the Member States: in spite of national differences, all Europeans face the same upheavals and the resulting threat to social cohesion.

Since the Commission considered the future of work to be at the heart of the much needed overhaul of the European social model, its departments decided, at the end of 1996, to pool their resources and work together for two years to achieve two things:

- First, to make the most of in-house knowledge in the quest for a solution to the unemployment problem;
- Second, to conduct an exploratory study to clarify the scope of the legal and financial decisions the European Union may soon be taking concerning social welfare and economic and social cohesion. After all, not all studies and suggestions are of equal value.

The *Carrefours des sciences et de la culture* had already outlined three approaches to reform based on different governing principles and involving different players:

- The first takes as its starting point the globalization of the economy and the spread of new forms of information technology. The conclusion is that, far from being on its last legs,

3

capitalism is evolving and becoming stronger. Some types of industry are gradually disappearing from Europe forever; these are being replaced by new tertiary activities and non-standard forms of work or organization. Our social structures are too rigid to allow us to take full advantage of the new forms of information technology, which are in fact already creating imbalances. It is important, therefore, that we help society adjust to the new order.

- The second concentrates on the shattering of social relations and regulatory systems. The solidarity, which would traditionally have existed between generations, regions or social groupings, has been eroded by the constant need to update work skills (lifelong learning) and new production techniques (teleworking). Artificial job creation is failing to create a new and lasting economic and social balance. This is a very serious and unprecedented situation that calls for drastic solutions – the redistribution of wealth and work.

- The third approach brings an ecological aspect to the debate (our development model is not sustainable), and a personal one – increasing incursions into free time threaten our personal equilibrium and survival. It calls for radical – some would say utopian – changes. But it also recommends that we pay heed to the positive trends that may emerge as the constraints once imposed by the organization of industrial work are removed. And it takes due note of the signs that work is already losing the central position it once occupied in our societies.

At the same time, it is clear from experiments carried out in Europe (the Netherlands, Sweden and Denmark) and elsewhere (Chile, New Zealand, the United States, Canada etc.) that recognition of the structural changes required does not rule out making particular choices about the kind of society we want to live in. It is essential, therefore, to highlight the advantages and disadvantages of each option by accurately assessing the consequences.

It quickly became clear from discussions within the Commission how difficult it was to find one's way around such a complex debate and the abundant literature that has been produced on the subject in recent years. First of all, therefore, it was necessary to:

- get an overview of all the various theories;
- find out how the public in the Member States are reacting; and
- establish what arguments are going round.

So as not to skew the exercise by opting for a particular approach or school of thought, no fewer than three reviews of the literature were commissioned from researchers chosen for their knowledge of particular groups of European countries:

- Nordic countries: Finnish researchers Pertti Koistinen and Ari Nieminen;
- Mediterranean countries: French researcher François Beaujolin;
- English-speaking countries: Berlin experts Jacqueline O'Reilly and Claudia Spee.

Similarly, to give equal emphasis to the three aspects of change now under way, each group of researchers was selected on the basis of their area of specialization:

- the workplace and other human activities in society: Pertti Koistinen and Ari Nieminen;
- technology, economics and the organization of work: François Beaujolin;
- social regulation: Jacqueline O'Reilly and Claudia Spee.

However, theories put forward in the debate on the future of work are often rejected as being too utopian. So it was also essential for the experts on European practice to check whether – as most of the authors claimed – actual examples of changed professional behaviour and new attitudes to work were to be found in local experiments. Of course, local development and employment initiatives (ILDEs), identified by the Commission as a promising means of creating jobs to fulfil new needs, are an attempt to break away from the standardized and fragmentary approach to job creation. They place job creation at the centre of a larger project designed to improve the quality of life or encourage local solidarity. It was, none the less, necessary to check methodically whether these initiatives were really a foretaste of the 'society without work'. The exploratory survey, conducted with the help of the *Centre de Recherche et d'Information sur la Démocratie et l'Autonomie* (Paris), associated with the French Scientific Research Council (CNRS), covered a sample of seven British and French projects regarded as particularly representative.

The first part of this paper contains individual and comparative analyses of these four studies. Summaries of the main body of the work and an indicative bibliography are annexed.

Finally – and this is not the least of the problems facing the European Commission – reforms aimed at shifting the boundary between work and leisure and constructing a new system capable of withstanding the centrifugal force of social exclusion cannot be decreed by a central authority. They have to be built up gradually through a democratic process involving all sections of civil society. The European Social Forum, which brings together the social partners and collective organizations, is an ideal environment in which to test ideas, assess their prevalence and start a joint building process. A summary of the debate (in the second part) classifies potential areas of Community action according to their timeframe.

This study on the future of work takes its inspiration from the work carried out over the last few years at the European Commission, under the supervision of the Forward Studies Unit (Marjorie Jouen) and DGV (Patrick Venturini and Ralf Jacob). It is based on a report written by Patrice Sauvage (consultant in socio-economics), supervised by Marjorie Jouen and Bénédicte Caremier, of the Forward Studies Unit.

PART I

The future of work according to the scientific literature

Can work, especially salaried work, which has shaped western societies since the industrial revolution, continue to play its traditional role now that millions of people are out of work, at least in Europe? Should it go on being the basis for social cohesion? If so, what policies should be followed to ensure that as many people as possible have a job? Or should that hope just be abandoned? But then what is to replace it? Finding answers to these questions is a vital stage in the designing of the European social model, which, together with the economic and monetary aspects, is an essential part of European Union.

In the prolific literature in the field, clashes between members of the different schools of thought are commonplace. The Commission therefore felt it appropriate to keep a certain distance from these discussions, and take stock of the scientific studies that have appeared over the previous few years. The objective is to base eventual recommendations on thorough studies rather than ideological presupposition.

Three 'reviews' of the scientific literature were commissioned from researchers from France, Germany and Finland. Below is a summary of their various approaches (sociological, legal, economic and technological respectively), which should throw up some guidelines and recommendations for the Commission.

In the first instance, our aim is to extract the main insights from each of the three studies, in as consistent a manner as possible, and then to look in more detail at the cross-disciplinary questions they raise.

Chapter 1

The main insights from the scientific literature

The way in which work evolves in society depends firstly on economic and technological factors (1.1), which have major implications for society (1.2) and therefore call for new methods of regulation (1.3).

1.1. THE CONSEQUENCES OF CURRENT ECONOMIC DEVELOPMENT ON WORK (ECONOMIC AND TECHNOLOGICAL APPROACH)[1]

1.1.1. On the nature of work

A new model of productive organization has come into being over the last few years. It is one based on production standards and choice regarding supply. This has led people to question the boundaries set up around organizations and, in more general terms, the forms employment takes.

First, the need for a flexible response tends to favour the 'company-network' model, in which the 'network' is made up

---

[1] François Beaujolin, *Technological and economic issues related to the future of work*, Study for the European Commission, August 1997.

of financially independent businesses within the same value chain: each business specializes in its own core activity and is one link in a series of transactions with the others. This model seems bound to lead to a decline in regular employment in a large organization – as the key to social integration – the cement that held traditional societies together.

There are, however, organizational forces acting against this trend: there is some resistance to the disappearance of organizations because outsourcing brings its own risks and difficulties – so the global trend towards concentration appears to be continuing. Moreover, we are also seeing the emergence of new rules for co-operation between companies in the same industry or the same geographical location. This gives organizations a certain amount of stability, particularly as regards principals and first-level subcontractors.

There is a definite trend towards a watering-down, a blurring of the edges, of commercial entities, which makes collective bargaining more difficult and tends to make firms feel they have no responsibility towards their workers. But there seem to be genuine economic forces holding the phenomenon in check; it perhaps affects multinational companies more than small businesses. However, it poses a real threat to the sense of collective identity through work.

Second, – a related development – the traditional form of employment contract is breaking down. The information society casts doubt on certain basic assumptions concerning the nature of regular employment. Can we still assume a fixed place of work, set working hours and an open-ended contract? The challenge is so strong that some people are talking of the demise of salaried work.[2]

The future of work may belong to the self-employed – with commercial, rather than salary-based, contracts. There are also

---

[2] William Bridges, *JobShift*, Addison-Wesley, Reading 1994.

signs that work is becoming more individualized and autonomous, with teleworking an extreme and hotly debated example.

At the other end of the spectrum, new forms of co-ordination are emerging within organizations (concerted project management, horizontal co-operation, vertical stratification),[3] which run counter to this manifest individualization. Still, on balance, the notion of belonging through work now seems under threat. All of this contributes to greater job insecurity, which could be alleviated by much more systematic policies on lifelong learning and local policies for managing employment. However, these have not been forthcoming.

There are two forms of insecurity, which combine to undermine the sense of belonging through work. The first arises from the precarious situation of businesses, though there are limits on this, even from a purely economic viewpoint. The second form, directly concerning the individual, results from employment contracts that emphasize the autonomy of the individual, but makes it more difficult for him or her to stand up to customer demand for services advertised by firms.

For Beaujolin, as for many writers on economics, the best way of responding to this dual insecurity – work-related and economic – is to acquire individual qualifications. He argues that individuals must adjust to the new economic order by developing their skills and their capacity for working on their own.[4] He proposes the introduction of workplace and 'empowerment' training courses. This, he believes, is one answer to the highly controversial question of the end of work.

1.1.2. On the quantity of work

Is the prospect of 'the end of work' approaching for the simple reason that its increasing precariousness is reducing the part it

---

[3] Philippe Zarifian, *Quels modèles d'organisation pour l'industrie européenne*, L'Harmattan, Paris 1993.
[4] François Beaujolin, see above.

plays in social integration, or is it, more objectively, that there will no longer be enough work for everybody, given the emergence of a kind of 'job-free' growth? That is the argument put forward by many authors, particularly Jeremy Rifkin in his best-seller, *The End of Work*.[5] In considering these questions, a distinction needs to be drawn between the global problem of lack of work and the specific – but extremely serious – issue of under-qualified workers.

With regard to unemployment on a global scale, Beaujolin firstly stresses, echoing the Arthuis report,[6] that globalization, which implies constant relocation, plays a significant role in reducing employment in some areas: in France, there are between three and five million jobs under direct threat from relocation.

However, as various French and American studies show, most of the manufacturing capacity in industrialized countries is now concentrated in sectors which rely primarily on qualified staff and innovation and are not, therefore, under threat from relocation to low-wage countries, so the outlook on that front is not disastrous.

The second debate, on technological unemployment caused by the third industrial revolution, is more difficult to assess, however. In Rifkin's view, this industrial revolution differs from previous ones in that it has not led to the emergence of a new area of activity to replace traditional sectors where jobs are being lost: the 'overspill' crisis. If our socio-economic model doesn't change, we are, in his view, heading towards massive unemployment and, in any event, towards a society where work – a rarity – can no longer supply the links that hold society together.

---

[5] Jeremy Rifkin, *The End of Work*, G.P. Putman's Sons, New York 1995.

[6] Jean Arthuis, *Les Délocalisations et l'Emploi*, Editions d'Organisations, Paris 1993.

This study, which received a lot of media coverage in France, was produced by Senator Arthuis, who was Minister of Finance from 1995 to 1997. It brings previous studies on relocation, particularly work carried out in France and the USA, up to date.

This theory is criticized by economists such as R.M. Solow,[7] who points out that, contrary to Rifkin's view, the current growth in productivity is small. He also disagrees with J. Lesourne,[8] who argues that we are still a long way from satisfying all our needs. Other writers find that the main causes of the 'overspill' crisis are political and social rigidities, which could be eased by more effective public policies, such as the activation of passive expenditure.

J. Rifkin believes there are two solutions to the global work shortage:

- Expansion of the tertiary sector to provide the much-needed sponge to mop up the overspill. But wouldn't this, as D. Meda fears,[9] amount to accepting the division of the population into two groups: those capable of staying inside the system (knowledge specialists, symbolic analysts etc.) and everyone else?

- Cuts in working hours. However, the various studies that have been done have failed to show that this is a cure-all. We now know what the key elements should be in a policy designed to boost employment by reducing working hours. They are: local negotiation; partial compensation for salary loss; and measures to ensure social contributions have a neutral effect for a given time period. These effects can be significant, but they have proved to be insufficient by themselves to solve the problem of unemployment. In the real world, reducing working time is not so much an effective method of job creation as an instrument of social progress in itself.

---

[7] Robert M. Solow, *Problèmes et perspectives de la croissance économique*; in: *Scénarios pour l'emploi*, Economica, 1995.
[8] Jacques Lesourne, *Vérités et mensonges sur le chômage*, Odile Jacob, Paris 1997.
[9] Dominique Méda, *La littérature américaine sur le travail. Un aperçu à travers trois livres récents*, Miméo, 1997.

There may be no consensus on the subject of the end of work in general terms, but it is clear that there is a major difficulty when it comes to under-skilled workers. They are more threatened than others by:

- globalization, which affects precisely those industries where they work in very large numbers, and overspill, which, in its current form is leading to a situation in which there is only one job-creating sector: the knowledge-based sector. This may drive further wedges between workers.

There are other contributory factors. To start with, Beaujolin identifies the emergence of a type of skewed technical progress which discriminates against under-skilled workers (unlike technical progress up until now, which produced specialized workers), these new forms of technology go better together with skilled work and are more of a substitute for non-skilled work. R. Reich, in *The Work of Nations*,[10] brilliantly showed how 'symbolic analysts' or symbol manipulators were stealing a march on workers in routine production services. This theory is disputed, however, since, according to European studies,[11] the rate at which skilled workers have replaced unskilled workers has actually fallen over recent years: moreover, new technologies (particularly expert systems)[12] can actually lessen the need for qualifications and make work easier for unskilled workers.[13]

---

[10] Robert Reich, *The Work of Nations*, Vintage Books, New York 1997.

[11] Jacques Drèze, Henri Sneesens, 'Progrès technique, mondialisation et travail peu qualifié'; in: *Pour l'emploi, la croissance et l'Europe*, Ed. de Boeck Université, Bruxelles 1995.

[12] Programmes designed to solve specific problems using experience acquired in a specialized field and directing the search for solutions (definition translated from *Le Petit Larousse*).

[13] OECD, *Technologie, productivité et création d'emploi*, Paris 1996.

Another question, which has been debated for a long time, is the level of pay for low-skilled workers. The Organisation for Economic Co-operation and Development (OECD), which campaigned for a lower minimum wage for a long time, particularly for young people, has become more cautious over the years; the various studies in the field have often produced conflicting conclusions, particularly since the end of the 1980s. Other factors, such as the overall level of demand and of the training received, are actually more important, it concludes.

In Beaujolin's view, one of the most telling reasons for the plight of low-skilled workers is the disparity between education and employment: according to the proponents of the disparity theory,[14] early training can produce over-qualified workers which the productive system cannot then accommodate. Added to that is the phenomenon of people taking up jobs for which they are over-qualified (too many graduates), keeping less qualified workers out of jobs for which their skills would have been adequate. Beaujolin maintains that these two factors are beyond dispute, unlike the preceding two (technological bias and level of minimum wage), on which the debate is still going on.

Despite the uncertainty over the minimum wage for workers, one of the solutions which has aroused most interest is reducing the cost of low-skilled labour, not through a reduction in the minimum wage, but by reducing employers' social security costs. The impact of such a measure, which may be significant, depends on the how the resulting deficit in social security funding is made up: some authors stress that a tax on capital or a steeper scale of social security contributions to offset it could have unpredictable effects and recommend caution in this regard.

Concluding his economy-based theory, Beaujolin emphasizes the problem of qualifications: the problem revolves around speed

---

[14] See the work of Louis Mallet in Europe and Edward N. Wolff in the United States.

of adjustment and mass transformation of workforce skills in developed countries, especially for low-skilled workers, to give them a chance of overcoming the obvious obstacles and finding a niche in this new pattern of development.

1.2. THE FRAGMENTATION OF WORK AND ITS SOCIAL CONSEQUENCES (SOCIOLOGICAL APPROACH)[15]

The fragmentation of work resulting from the present shortage and insecurity of work leads the authors of this review to question its place in society (1.2.1.), and then to concentrate on three relatively new subject areas which the crisis has brought to the fore: the integration of migrants, the new lifecycle and new forms of work, particularly in the non-market sector (1.2.2.). In the light of these developments, it is legitimate to ask what type of social infrastructure could afford protection for all in an increasingly uncertain society (1.2.3.).

1.2.1. Questioning the role of work in society

In surveying various studies on 'the end of work', Koistinen and Nieminen ask firstly if the whole of society is affected or if the problem is specific to certain disadvantaged groups: according to R. Dahrendorf's 'two-thirds society' theory, one third of the population is set to be excluded from work. In that case, the problem associated with work would primarily be the polarization between people with a lot of work and people with very little, and the social exclusion that would result. Hence the need for a new legal framework to guarantee the rights of citizens having to cope with the erosion of the traditional work model: it should

---

[15] Pertti Koistinen and Ari Nieminen. *Literature survey on the future of work*. Study for the European Commission, June 1997.

be remembered how much class conflicts shaped the industrial society and citizenship. New social divisions require an adjustment or, preferably, a reformulation of social rights to prevent whole sections of society from being marginalized. This reworking should recognize that differences are becoming more pronounced, as a result of the powerful market and competition culture, and it should attempt to reconcile this trend with the European tradition of solidarity.

In more general terms, salary and wage-earning work is losing its three essential functions:

- *Production:* other forms of production such as self-employment and co-operatives (plus freelance work – see study by Beaujolin) seem to be more efficient. More generally, the 'work' factor does not seem to be the main source of productivity any longer;
- *Distribution:* distribution of income and its redistribution through the social welfare system were traditionally achieved through salaried employment. The current fragmentation of this kind of work has undermined it as a basis for labour law and social rights (see *Manifeste pour une Europe sociale* published in 1996);[16]
- *Socialization:* since salaried work has become an essential means of identity building and social integration for men, and indeed women, there is a problem of socialization both for the increasing numbers of unemployed people and for those doing increasingly solitary and insecure jobs that have lost their collective dimension (see study by Beaujolin).

In other words, as salaried work continues to lose the significance it once had for the economy, and becomes increasingly uncertain and polarized, to the detriment of specific social categories (under-skilled workers and migrants – see above), we should start

---

[16] Ulrich Mückenberger, Brian Bercusson, Simon Deakin, Pertti Koistinen, Yota Kravariton, Alain Supiot, Bruno Veneziani, *Manifeste pour une Europe sociale*, Ed. Desclée de Brouwer, 1996.

thinking about a new social contract. Our aim must be to ensure that these developments do not damage cohesion in our societies.

1.2.2. Three emerging themes

The problem outlined above becomes still more if the following three issues are factored in – and, the European social model being what it is, they cannot be left out:

The migrant issue

The migrant issue is an illustration of the point that market-driven differentiation and the European welfare tradition have to be reconciled. Migration flows triggered by globalization also make for greater diversity and increased job insecurity. The International Labour Organisation (ILO) stresses that we are now seeing 'temporary immigration', which is creating an 'ethnic underclass'. Should we simply acquiesce in this state of affairs or encourage a new form of solidarity towards migrants?

To start with, the ILO's international agreements, particularly the one on undeclared employment, should be enforced more strictly. Then we should start thinking about current policy in European countries that emphasize the residence criterion while making it more difficult to gain entry. Citizenship as a concept is actually devalued by comparison with residence, the only major factor in determining whether the holder gains access to social rights and equality before the law. But shouldn't the European Union guarantee citizenship for everyone who lives and works in Europe?

Taking the situation in Sweden as an example, Koistinen and Nieminen stress the need for what they call pluralist integration, based on a type of development that favours diversity rather than social differentiation. Socially advanced though Sweden is, the unemployment rate for migrants is still 2.5 times that of the indigenous population. In addition to the economic and technological reasons for this, there are cultural factors at play: ethnic and cultural diversity is seen there as a threat to the social order. Shouldn't such diversity be seen rather as an asset to be deliberately invested in? This should be the focus of future policies in the area.

The shifting meaning of work throughout an individual's life

The shifting meaning of work throughout an individual's life is the second phenomenon tackled by the sociological literature. The first observation is that there is a new relationship between life at work and life outside work. Working life is shorter and more unstable, whereas retirement has become a time for activity; we move from a linear life model (education → active life → retirement) to an alternating or overlapping model in which people switch from one phase to another in the course of their lives (A. Suikkanen and L. Viinamäki).[17]

This is why a new type of social protection is needed, no longer based on the idea of protection from risk but designed primarily to facilitate the switches between the various phases, which can occur several times during a life cycle.

However, active retirement is the question that interests our two Scandinavian consultants most. In their view, a distinction should be made between retired people who are still young and likely to be active and those who, for health reasons, are to be seen more as consumers (of the services they depend on, in particular). In view of the serious problems with funding pensions, and the creative capacity of the people concerned, middle-aged people should be integrated as fully as possible into the labour market.

---

[17] Asko Suikkanen and Leena Viinamäki, Ending of work, life course and labour market citizenship. 18th conference on employment systems in Europe and the state of well-being, Tampere (Finland) 9–14 July 1996.

The ageing population is the most important change to consider: while the elderly are in better health than ever, they are still discriminated against in the jobs market. That must stop.

Several suggestions are made for adapting the work process to ageing workers: training in information technology, developing autonomous areas of action and control within companies and, more fundamentally, promoting lifelong learning.

We need a policy that covers life as a whole, not just work. Is there a way of setting up a partnership between society, firms and individuals that would provide a healthy way of life for everyone, both at work and at home?

The need to break down the market/non-market dichotomy

This brings us back to the need to break down the market/non-market dichotomy, an issue examined in greater depth in the study by O'Reilly and Spee (see 1.3) and the centre de recherche et d'information sur la démocratie et l'autonomie – CRIDA.[18] The authors first highlight the emergence of new forms of employment linked to local initiatives, measures to reduce unemployment and the reorganization of the public sector to cater for the new demand for services. Are we heading towards the establishment of a 'third sector', as Rifkin hopes, or are we running the risk (identified by Beaujolin, among others) of increasing social polarization?

The division of labour between housework and community work is then discussed. The growing number of women in the workforce leaves a sizeable area of domestic work that women are either no longer inclined or able to do, and this opens up enough job opportunities to alleviate unemployment. The question of overspill plays a role here: each country will develop these activities in its own way, according to its culture and history. The consultants emphasize the difficulties facing Scandinavian

---

[18] See Point 3.4, Part 1.

countries, which are used to the idea of public services being provided by public institutions.

Like C. Labruyère,[19] the authors emphasize the strict distinction that must be made between the two categories of home worker:

- Employees whose work is very similar to traditional domestic work but who have a commercial relationship with several families;
- Home helps, who are more akin to social workers or paramedics and are employed by home-help agencies. In view of the enormous range of potential jobs in this sector, it is important to provide social protection for these two categories of vulnerable workers.

1.2.3. What does the future hold for work?

Four subject areas are grouped below. For each, we either make practical proposals or recommend avenues of research.

Support for people

With all the changes going on in society, this is a priority. Koistinen and Nieminen point in particular to the specific problems faced by the children of the unemployed, particularly if they belong to minority ethnic groups or if their parents are long-term unemployed. Their situation must not be allowed to jeopardize their chances of social integration, or stop them developing a positive self-image. Even if some studies pay little attention to these types of problems, efforts should be made to ensure that the children concerned are given the same care and services as others.

---

[19] C Labruyère, *Les services aux personnes à domicile: problème de professionnalisation.* Formation et Emploi, CEREQ Newsletter 1997.

In more general terms, since the future is becoming increasingly uncertain and employers now have much greater power, workers are under heavy pressure and are having to live with stress and insecurity. Individuals need to be made to feel secure in their own identity and unions and workers' associations need to pay more heed to the plight of people working in insecure jobs. Here, Koistinen and Nieminen echo the conclusions of Beaujolin's study in proposing action to promote new qualifications, but with the emphasis on social-skills training in the framework of learning organizations rather than just strictly vocational qualifications.

So new forms of social support and dialogue need to be developed within companies and in their environment. Will the various partners concerned be capable of reaching agreement on a long-term, innovative policy for the working environment? The answer to this question is of fundamental importance for the future of the European social model.

Redistribution of work: An option for European societies

Even if, as we saw above, the effects of sharing work are hotly disputed and, in the end, relatively minor, it is one of the more promising options for Europe, where a high value has traditionally been placed on solidarity. The objective must be to strike a better balance between productive and reproductive work (see study by O'Reilly and Spee), to share productive work out more fairly between workers and the unemployed and to make sure there is a more even distribution of work, rest and leisure throughout the life cycle.

The authors' most telling argument for research and experimentation in this area in Europe is the change in attitudes. In Scandinavian countries, at least, a majority of people are interested in work sharing: this shift in values, which is consistent with Europe's fundamental cultural precepts (solidarity, equality, quality of life), should be the guiding principle as policies in the area are explored further.

Standardization and differentiation

In one respect, as the economy becomes a global one, we are seeing a pattern of development unfurl which tends towards standardization, described by G. Ritzler as 'Mc Donaldization'. 'The American way of life'[20] he says, is gradually strengthening its grip on the whole world. However, the authors stress that employment systems still vary widely from country to country in Europe, in line with their cultural values, traditions and social structures. All the policies to be formulated have to fit into the particular framework of each Member State: that is where the difficulty with a European policy in this area lies, faced with the 'steamroller' of the globalized economy.[21]

Another topic which Koistinen and Nieminen think could be looked at here is the 'return of social classes'. In his book 'Repositioning Class',[22] Gordon Marshall points out that an analysis in terms of social stratification is still relevant, provided that concepts such as the meritocracy, social exclusion ('underclass') and the relations between classes and the sexes are included.

Encouraging fresh confidence in a new social contract

All the authors studied for the purposes of this sociological review agreed emphatically on the need for a new vision of work and employment. However, this must be based on a new social contract which, in turn, relies on mutual trust among the various

---

[20] George Ritzer, *The McDonaldization Thesis – Explorations and Extensions*, Sage Publications, 1988.

[21] We will return to this point in the second part of this summary.

[22] Gordon Marshall, *Repositioning Class – Social Inequality in Industrial Societies*, Sage Publications, 1997.

players: this, it appears, gives the Scandinavian countries a competitive advantage. More importantly, the authors stress that informal rules and ways of speaking – 'unofficial' ways of behaving, in other words – have a vital part to play over and above legal regulations and official agreements.

Current research is too 'rationalistic', for example as regards work sharing: this, they say, requires new attitudes for which the classic 'homo oeconomicus' is not known. Human sciences reach their limit at this point, but several studies, such as the one by F. Fukuyama,[23] have begun to explore this area, which has been ignored for too long.

1.3. HOW SHOULD WORK AND WELFARE BE REGULATED? (INSTITUTIONAL APPROACH)[24]

This study is shorter and engages with the issues more than previous ones. It attempts to provide a deeper understanding of the problems with regulation by looking at the whole picture, in a general review of the social contract and relations between the sexes.

Traditional studies in this field have confined themselves to the productive domain and, therefore, to the masculine model of work. A more integrated approach is needed, in the framework of what the authors call 'employment systems'. These cover three interdependent areas:

- economic production (companies);
- social reproduction (home life);
- regulation (public authorities).

---

[23] Francis Fukuyama, *Trust: The Social Virtues and the Creation of Prosperity*, Free Press, New York 1995.

[24] Jacqueline O'Reilly and Claudia Spee, *Regulating work and welfare of the future: Towards a new social contract or a new gender contract?* Study for the European Commission, September 1997.

On the basis of this model, different European employment systems can be described and a better understanding gained of trends regarding the regulation of work and social welfare.

1.3.1. The regulation of work

All the authors agree there is a general tendency towards greater flexibility, but it is interesting to note that this tendency can operate at four separate levels: national, industry, company and individual. Taking these as our criteria, we can distinguish three ways of regulating work:

- *Statist flexibility* (France and Spain): The key element here is the workers' status, negotiated at national level. In France, the power of employers is on the increase, whereas in Spain a better balance is being struck between management and unions.
- *Negotiated flexibility* (Sweden and Germany) – between management and labour at the individual industry level: There is little state intervention in this system, which has served as a model for others for a long time, but it is now running into difficulties, especially in Germany, where it relies far too heavily on the masculine model of full-time work. A less corporatist and more decentralized approach seems to be needed, as in the Netherlands, where a greater salary spread has been accepted and part-time work is encouraged.
- *Individualized flexibility* – where the onus is on individuals: Since the Thatcher years, this is the predominant model in the United Kingdom, which remains hostile to any form of European harmonization and which provides poor protection for workers in atypical employment.[25]

---

[25] For example, there is much less protection for part-time workers than in France or Spain.

However work is regulated, there is still a common trend in all these countries towards decentralization and flexible production processes, which reduces the rights of permanent employees everywhere.

In these circumstances, can there be a trade-off between work flexibility and job protection, following the example of the Netherlands, where the concept of 'flexicurity' is being tested? Dutch legislation increases the rights of temporary workers by reducing the rights of permanent workers. This means that 'security within a job' is replaced by 'job security'. However, it is doubtful whether this model – which some say gives too much weight to flexibility – can be adapted to suit other countries. There has to be something to negotiate.

Another attempt to make a trade-off between flexibility and security is the French legislation on the reduction of working time (the Robien Law adopted in June 1996 and the Aubry Law of 13 June 1998). The controversy these laws unleashed prompts O'Reilly and Spee to suggest that it is more difficult for statist regulation systems to bring off such an exchange than for negotiated flexibility systems. As for the British system, it would seem to lead inevitably to a widening of the gap between rich and poor.

So what will happen at European level?

P. Lange[26] thinks it unlikely that we will see the emergence of a 'social democratic Europe' which applies this kind of trade-off generally. Instead, we can expect a pluralistic approach to social policy in Europe, with pronounced national variations and a few common regulations. New forms of work regulation, particularly those regarding the role of part-time work, will have to be incorporated into the various employment systems.

---

[26] Peter Lange, The politics of the social dimension; in: A.M. Sbragia (ed.), *Europolitics. Institutions and Policymaking in the 'new' European Community*, Brooking Institute, Washington 1992.

J. Rubery[27] highlights the danger that developing part-time work could damage the rights of full-time workers. O'Reilly and Spee think it might be better to tackle this subject in conjunction with social reproduction, since the topic of part-time work brings us back to the question of different stages in our lives and domestic matters. In other words, our thinking on part-time work and the reduction of working hours should be set in the wider context of how we live our lives.

1.3.2. The regulation of social welfare

Like employment systems in the strict sense, systems of social regulation have been shaped by history and there is very little convergence between them at present.

On the basis of three criteria – 'decommodification' (the degree of state intervention in the distribution of income), stratification based on social class and relations between the state and the market, G. Esping-Andersen[28] has classified 18 countries in terms of liberal, conservative and social democratic types. These different types of welfare state have distinct implications for the labour market, particularly as regards women.

Social integration of women is stronger where the state plays a larger role, firstly as a provider of childcare, which gives women greater access to work, and, secondly, as a provider of public service jobs, which are more oriented towards women than those in the private sector.

---

[27] Jill Rubery, Part-time work: A threat to labour standards; in: J. O'Reilly and J. Fagan (ed.), *Part-time Prospects*, Routledge, London 1998.

[28] Gosta Esping-Andersen, *The Three Worlds of Welfare Capitalism*, Polity Press, Cambridge 1990.

In this way, the authors substitute the male/female divide for the division between social classes as the focal point for studying the systems of regulation in Europe. Several researchers categorize such systems according to whether they give priority to the traditional 'male breadwinner' model – division of labour between the man earning the wages and the woman at home dependent on her spouse. The United Kingdom and Germany are the countries where the male breadwinner model is most prevalent, while the Scandinavian countries are where it is least prevalent, with France situated somewhere between the two.

Reviewing various studies with sometimes more sophisticated methods of classification, O'Reilly and Spee stress the considerable differences between systems of social regulation, which lead inevitably to different paths of development: it seems unlikely, therefore, that such systems will ever converge. Two current trends illustrate this point.

In the first instance, there is a general trend towards the development of partnerships between the public and private sectors for the provision of services traditionally supplied by the State. The increase in the number of unemployed and elderly people, and the need for the State to reduce its deficits has led, almost everywhere, to the introduction of more market-oriented solutions, tailored to the specific needs of consumers. For example, such solutions have been adopted by public employment agencies in several countries (Austria, Germany and the Netherlands) using a three-way model (incorporating employers and labour).

These innovations may, however, have their disadvantages: lower quality service and failure to cater for the neediest cases because of the cost and complexity. Several researchers have questioned the preference for action at local level – which many countries think is the best level for interaction between economic and social factors. Isn't the role of action at local level overestimated, in comparison with the structural implications of national and supranational institutions? In other words, is local management of employment an effective means of action or merely a palliative?

This trend may be a common thread in drawing European countries together, but they differ greatly in their approach to implementation: on one extreme, the United Kingdom extends market principles to all services provided to individuals; on the other, Sweden and the Netherlands are simply modernizing their public sectors. Seen from the feminist perspective of the researchers, privatization generally works against integration of women into the labour market. According to M. Oppen,[29] this is what is happening in the new German *Länder*.

The second common trend is the introduction of new ways of providing services with a social benefit aspect, such as service vouchers or work pools. The aim is to professionalize and legitimize new activities and thereby create 'transitional' labour markets, which would constitute just one step in the integration process rather than the end of that process. However, despite the often encouraging results of these experiments, might there not be a risk of perpetuating the fragmentation of the labour market and creating a low-paid category of work mainly performed by women?

The point at issue here is the type of relationship that should be set up between work flexibility, services with a social benefit dimension, social security protection and risk. Some suggest the answer should be a citizenship allowance or a negative tax, a notion that they say urgently needs to be introduced into the debate.

In conclusion, the social contract has failed to incorporate the high-risk groups and ought to be reviewed. Above all, it must take account of the gender divide, which has been largely disregarded until now because of the prevalence of the 'male breadwinner' model. If this is to happen, the principle of equality, based on the masculine standards of individual merit and citizenship, will have to be yoked together with the idea of difference, which

---

[29] Maria Oppen, Modernisierung als Privatisierung; in: *Das Argument*, 204/1994.

takes greater account of the family responsibilities that have, until now, largely fallen to women. There is often a blind spot in studies on this issue: the issue of whether there should be closer ties between the feminist movement and the unions.

The second aim of this new contract should be to prevent social polarization: faced with the trend towards deregulation, the authors feel it would be possible to update labour market regulations rather than watering them down, thereby enhancing the quality of work currently regarded as atypical. However, this preventative policy should concern not just the labour market, but also social reproduction and welfare regulation: a holistic approach through which a new contract between men and women could be constructed.

Chapter 2

The terms of the debate

What can we conclude from the three approaches we have just outlined? Here in Chapter 2, we will take a broader approach, starting from the four questions that prompted the European Commission to ask for this survey:

1) Can we expect a change in the meaning of work in society as well as a change in the nature of work? Or are the radical changes currently being discussed greatly overrated, or simply belied by the facts?
2) Isn't the challenge, then, to hold society together by helping as many as possible of the people excluded by existing employment systems (back) onto the labour market?
3) What social groups are the most dynamic – those most likely to bring about change, as the partners in a new social contract?
4) In the light of the above, what are the priority changes to be made to social infrastructures? What policies would deliver the greatest incentives and the most protection?

What can be said at the end of this first part of the summary is that the third question goes largely unanswered in the scientific literature.[30] However, it has been extensively debated in the

---

[30] Except in a very general manner in the article by Jacqueline O'Reilly and Claudia Spee on the various systems of employment and welfare and the public/private link.

European social forum.[31] We shall, therefore, deal with the other three questions, where the studies did make some progress, though they left them largely unresolved. At least they clarified the terms of the debate to which Europe's leaders will have to address themselves.

2.1. THE FUTURE OF WORK

What conclusions can be drawn from these studies regarding changes in the nature of work, and the amount of work available for the purpose of integrating as many people as possible into society? The conclusions are, to a large extent, qualified, which means that neither a fatalistic nor a utopian vision of the problem prevails.

2.1.1. How far should we go with the change in work?

Economic authors have described the current trend towards the individualization of work and increasing job insecurity. Aside from the problem of low-skilled workers, which is tackled later on, the question arises as to the limits of the process of individualization. Beaujolin draws attention to some 'automatic stabilisers', as he calls them, which prevent the system from descending into total anarchy, either in specific industries or production units. The question is also whether such analyses are valid for small and very small businesses, which are playing an increasingly vital role in creating employment.

As the three studies point out, these processes may be limited quite simply by the very people concerned, who have to put up with increasing stress and insecurity and whose apparent productivity may be undermined by new types of work-related illness.[32]

---

[31] See Part 2.
[32] See Christophe Dejours, *Souffrance en France*, Seuil 1998.

This type of increasingly competitive work puts pressure on men, and even more on women, whose integration through work may be seriously jeopardized by the strength of market forces (see O'Reilly and Spee's analysis).

What is to be done? The answers given in the studies, or emerging from them, can be divided into three categories, ranging from the micro to the macro level, i.e.:

- provide better support for individuals, not just in terms of qualifications, but also in terms of personal development, so that they can 'adapt to change';
- promote solidarity between local firms (e.g. employers' groupings, work pools) and territorial management of work, which would remove some of the insecurity from the labour market by providing people with coherent career paths;
- give the whole process a thorough overhaul, rather than trying to adapt people to it or alleviate the consequences at local level. O'Reilly and Spee think that it would be possible, at European level, to modernize labour law without going all out for flexibility, which would weaken the rights of all workers.

The question is whether Europe, after the establishment of economic and monetary union, will have the resources – and whether it wishes to use them as part of its social policy – to put a halt to this creeping job insecurity which, as the Finnish authors point out, flies in the face of its values of solidarity (including solidarity between men and women). What balance should it strike between the much-needed adaptation of its labour force to international competition and the social cohesion it sees as vital?

As we saw in the third review of the literature, each country will have to find solutions to suit its own particular employment system. But there is still a need to develop a joint approach at European level. The approach should have two strands, in proportions influenced by global trends:

- a programme to bring individuals and countries into line with the new configuration of work;[33]
- deliberate steps to set limits to the undermining of job security, which runs counter to the European social model.

2.1.2. 'Putting a stop to the end of work'[34]

With regard to the amount of work available, J. Rifkin's theory on the 'end of work' is quoted by the authors we are looking at, though they only partially subscribe to it. Beaujolin notes that the globalization of the economy has undoubtedly affected employment in the industrialized countries, but that its impact has remained moderate. On unemployment due to technology, which lies at the core of Rifkin's argument, the discussion is, unfortunately, rather confused. Also, a recent ILO study[35] shows that in Europe, over the last few years, growth has brought with it an unprecedented rise in employment and that the current unemployment problem is mainly due to the increase in the size of the active population, creating a supply of work surplus to demand, even though a considerable number of jobs are being created. Furthermore, as Beaujolin points out, qualifications are still not adapting fast enough to our current pattern of growth. According to these studies, there is no sign of an imminent end to work – on the contrary, there may even be labour shortages in certain European countries in a few years' time.[36]

---

[33] This could be seen, in a more positive light, as an 'appropriation' of the new forms of work by people and territories.

[34] To use Anne-Marie Grozelier's term in *Pour en finir avec la fin du travail*, Ed. de l'atelier, Paris 1997.

[35] ILO report on world employment 1996–1997, Chapter 2, 'Is full employment a thing of the past?'.

[36] In Sweden, according to a study carried out by the National Employment Agency, shortages may occur in the education, health and building sectors (*Infor MISEP*, No 63, Autumn 1998, page 33).

While the 'end of work' theory needs to be put into context, there remains the problem of 'overspill' raised by Rifkin; very slow, uphill progress is being made towards new job-creating activities. The studies provide us with some very helpful insights, pointing out that there can be no single answer to the problem: while the United States tackles the problem through a market-oriented approach and deregulation, European countries must first find solutions which are consistent with their histories and values. Neither Sweden nor France, which both have a strong statist tradition (and a good record on the integration of women into the workforce owing to public-service postings), can rely solely on market-related measures for the introduction of inter-personal and local services.

Secondly, as the Finnish and German studies point out, the emergence of these new types of activity should not be used as a pretext for further polarization. The sector must not become a haven for a new sort of underpaid 'domestic service'. A great deal of effort will have to be put into developing solid qualifications and labour law to bring credibility to the sector. This may provide an opportunity to overhaul the co-operative sector in its present form and move towards Rifkin's 'third sector'. The current work on local initiatives and Europe's solidarity-based economy go some way towards this.[37]

Getting the conditions right for this overspill to occur will require time. Leaving it entirely to the market is an inappropriate solution for many countries, but are they prepared to take the time, as their values dictate, to invest in these new kinds of activity and accept a higher unemployment rate for a great many years to come?

Another solution put forward by Rifkin is job-sharing. The various studies pulled together by Beaujolin illustrate the limited

---

[37] See article by CRIDA on local development and employment initiatives (Part 2).

job-creating powers of this solution. Even so, as Koistinen and Nieminen show, such a policy would be more consistent with European values and what people in Europe want than total deregulation of the market along American lines. In that area too, we should take our time, because the best way to make progress is to decentralize negotiations as much as possible (O'Reilly and Spee), which explains the difficulties faced by countries with flexible state-directed systems.[38]

There is also the proposal made by Rifkin, among others, for a citizenship allowance or a negative tax. This solution, which has been widely debated, particularly in France, is only mentioned briefly by the German and Finnish researchers. The role regular employment plays in society is undoubtedly set to diminish (see Koistinen and Nieminen), but the prospect of the link between work and income being broken appears very distant. Without really discussing this hypothesis, the authors argue implicitly that work should continue to play a major role in income distribution and the shaping of individual identity. Also, according to the CRIDA article, the point of local development and employment initiatives is not to question the salaried-work model but to entrench it more securely.[39]

Of course the boundaries between paid work and the non-market and social reproduction spheres should no longer been seen as rigidly fixed; salaried work should be looked at in the wider context of lifestyle, but that does not make it any less necessary (or possible) to get as many people as possible into, or back into, work.

We should, then, drop the fatalistic approach: the tendency towards greater flexibility can only go so far before it runs up against organizational and economic limits, which should, with

---

[38] In this connection, it would be very interesting to explore the French experiment in reducing working time launched by Martine Aubry, which amounts to a call on the social partners to negotiate.

[39] See Part 2.

luck mean that firms will not go too far; second, not enough work has been done at the level of individuals and regions, where the capacity for adjustment and creativity might serve as another 'automatic stabiliser'; finally, since Europe is keen to preserve its model of civilization, it should not balk at setting limits to a process that could undermine its social cohesion.

As regards the second debate about 'the end of work', Rifkin seems to be jumping to conclusions. It is true that the significance of salaried work is diminishing, to judge by the literature at any rate. This is a welcome development because it has for too long been the mainstay of personal identity and social integration. However, the demographic outlook in Europe, the major policy of facilitating overspill of jobs into new activities and further movement in the long-standing trend towards shorter working hours – they will all help us to solve the overall unemployment problem by 2010.

2.2. EXCLUDED FROM WORK

In reality, if there is to be an 'end to work', it mainly concerns a number of 'high-risk' social groups which, given the emphasis in today's economy on excellence and adaptability, do not have the skills to find jobs. The main exclusion factor is low qualifications, but there are others: ethnic origin (see references to migrants in the study by Koistinen and Nieminen), age (see comments by Beaujolin on the middle-aged), and sex (see study by O'Reilly and Spee).

2.2.1. A fundamental challenge for Europe

There is clearly a contradiction between:

- the conclusion reached in the preceding point, in favour of a long-term job-creation and job-sharing strategy in the expectation that the active population in Europe will start to shrink in the next few years; and

- the urgent need for action to address the acute problem of social polarization associated with long-term unemployment and ethnic exclusion. This weighs heavily on individuals and also on their children (Koistinen and Nieminen), jeopardising their chances of social integration. As work must, at least for the foreseeable future, continue to be an important factor in social integration and identity, the most important goal of employment policies in Europe is to get people into (or back into) work.

We cannot accept a mere trade-off between less effective protection for permanent workers and greater compensation for people excluded from the labour market or with insecure jobs. There have to be better solutions than that most basic redistribution from the 'work-rich' to the 'work-poor'. On the one hand, of course, the surplus will indeed have to be redistributed, not just in the form of monetary compensation but in less tangible forms of support for individuals (training, personalized help, etc.). At the same time, though, we should be asking more fundamental questions about the way the economy works, to prevent certain groups being excluded in the first place. Here, Beaujolin, and Koistinen and Nieminen make two valid proposals:

- They suggest a review of human-resource management methods in companies and set up schemes to draw on the experience of older workers and the practical know-how of the lower-skilled. There are ways of doing this which are just as profitable to companies as the traditional approaches which generate exclusion, but they require a significant amount of extra organization;
- At a more basic level – and this is particularly relevant to migrant workers and women, whose relationship to work is different from men's – we should promote an economy based on diversity, where diversity is not seen as a handicap but as an attribute which brings something to the whole community.

This means developing economic activities, even if these are not profitable, to give the people concerned a chance of displaying the qualities which they possess but which are currently undervalued by our economic system: this is the object of several local employment and integration initiatives and they deserve more support.

However, moves such as these will not solve the problem quickly, as they will entail substantial cultural changes. Recruitment subsidies, which produce the familiar windfall effect, also have their limits, of course. So, if action is to be taken rapidly to stop a sizeable percentage of the active population getting trapped in a state of exclusion, the only solution left is to cut the cost of unskilled labour, though not by lowering the minimum wage (a solution which even the Organization for Economic Co-operation and Development (OECD) now rejects), but by cutting the social security costs on low salaries. According to the studies analysed by Beaujolin, this will not solve all the problems, but it could, if there is the political will and effective planning, produce significant results.

Finally, it is surprising to find no mention in these studies of the famous workfare schemes tried out in the United States and the United Kingdom. While it would seem that the aspects of this system involving constraint and apportioning of blame should be rejected, it does have the advantage of rapidly finding work for people who might otherwise be shut out of the labour market for good, or keeping them in work. Tony Blair's experiment in this field should be monitored carefully to see if it can produce any conclusions consistent with continental European values.

2.2.2. Specific groups

We have already alluded to the problem of temporary immigration, which is tending to produce an ethnic underclass. What we see clearly here are the extremes of a process of increasing job uncertainty, which hits this category of the population particularly hard and ought to concern the European Union, as it leads to serious breakdowns in its social cohesion. Koistinen and Nieminen do touch on this subject, but the European Commission should look at it in more detail, going beyond the 'protectionist' standpoint of the Schengen agreements and with an eye to potential labour shortages that could make immigration even more necessary. Surely this should be tackled on a sounder basis.

It may come as a surprise to hear elderly workers and women described as being potentially excluded from work. Early retirement for the elderly is a convenient way of removing them from the labour market which has been used by a number of countries for a long time to 'make room' for others. However, it is suicidal in the light of current population trends. This is why Koistinen and Nieminen think an all-out effort is required to keep older people in the workforce or even bring them back.

A more liberal approach to work, however, including voluntary work, seems more appropriate. Voluntary work carried out by comparatively young retired people is also very helpful in making new job-creating activities possible.

Where women are concerned, unless they go back to the home to 'make room for others', as some in responsible positions would like them to, they pay the highest price in terms of insecure work, in the form of part-time work and the low-grade jobs which constitute the 'new domestic service' (see O'Reilly and Spee). Rather than restricting the part they play in the economy, they should be encouraged to get involved so that the prevailing systems, based on the masculine model, can be given a holistic overhaul and expanded to include social reproduction.

If we are to make it easier for these groups to play a part, we will need a society of full activity: this means breaking down the barriers between traditional salaried work, new forms of employment in the co-operative sector and the non-market economy, while trying to ensure that this diversification of work and activity does not lower individual living standards, but actually gives people greater opportunities for development. This, by and large, is the vision espoused by several local development and employment initiatives looked at by CRIDA: a massive challenge for Europe, but a worthwhile ambition for the European social model.

2.3. WHAT SOCIAL MODEL SHOULD EUROPE ADOPT?

Various proposals for policies and 'social infrastructures' have been outlined. Let us now see how they relate to the two fundamental challenges for the European social model identified in the studies.

The first question European leaders should be asking themselves after reading these surveys of the literature on work is whether European society should adjust to the present economic circumstances and its repercussions for work or whether the rules of the game can be changed. Can the economy be reformed to prevent it 'going against society'?[40]

If reforms are on the cards, what direction should they take? Should we be looking for ways of increasing the number of salaried jobs or scaling down their relative importance? This is the second question that needs to be answered.

2.3.1. Should we put up with the system or correct it?

Let us examine the alternatives before we start developing more refined approaches. The first option is to accept greater flexibility and greater job uncertainty, while trying to provide everyone with the means to adapt to that type of system. Here is a selection of the proposals that have been made along those lines:

---

[40] See Bernard Perret and Guy Roustang, *L'économie contre la société*, Seuil, Paris 1995.

- training and support for individuals (new qualifications, social skills);
- providing a safety net that is more suited to present economic circumstances: better cover for workers in insecure jobs, reduced social security contributions for low-paid workers, social cover which makes it easier to switch from one situation to another and which is not simply designed to offset risk;
- creation of transitory or occupational activities at local level.

The second option is a pluralist economy based on solidarity[41] – pluralist in the sense that:

- a single economic model must not be made to fit all countries, as each has its own traditions;
- business must attach greater value to difference and diversity (men, women, migrants etc.);
- the new sector of activity catering for overspill should not necessarily develop according to the laws of the market deregulation.

In other words, the relationship between unity and difference should be reversed: emphasis would be placed on the oneness of the individual and the diversity of the economy, in contrast to the current state of affairs, where the individual is brushed to one side by a monolithic economic structure). It is based on solidarity, in that the aim is to promote a more co-operative form of work organization, job-sharing and make firms take more responsibility for their social and geographical environment.

In practice, the choice between these two types of model is not as clear cut as it might seem.[42] Training and support for

---

[41] See OECD, *Réconcilier l'économique et le social – L'économie plurielle* OCDE – Poche No 12, 1996. Only in French.

[42] See Part 2, article on the debates at the European Social Forum which concluded that consensus was possible.

individuals must remain a priority. We need people with training, particularly in social skills, to develop a pluralist economy based on solidarity. Also, action at local level cannot be just a sop. It must form the basis for new links between economic and social issues, for the good of society as a whole. And even if we think the trend towards job insecurity can be reversed, immediate action is needed to remedy a system of social protection that discriminates against the lowest-skilled workers and those in the least secure jobs.

Given the potential strength of the competitive economy, which is heading towards even greater flexibility, Europe should help its society adjust to these economic circumstances. That is why more decentralized and individualized approaches are required, as the various studies point out.

But that should not be the end of it. It seems that Europe, given its economic strength, has the means not just to play the game well, but also to change the rules of the game, by promoting a mode of development more in line with its values. Instead of this relentless drive to open up new commercial frontiers and create the perfect environment for competition, which seems to obsess some European leaders, surely it would be preferable to invest in Europe's social dimension and in local job-creation initiatives which will create better conditions for 'overspill'.

2.3.2. What should the policy on work be?

The significance of salaried work may be steadily diminishing in economic terms but as we have seen, most authors do not seriously predict the 'end of work' as a frame of reference for personal identity, income distribution and social cohesion. Most experts agree on the importance of providing everyone with a job, whether by creating new types of activity or sharing available work ('workfare' also falls into this category).

However, the 'jobs for all' approach, which has not been pursued seriously enough in Europe, also has its limits, in that it relates only to salaried work. How far can we go in the commercialization of family and interpersonal relationships? Is job-sharing viable if it takes no account of 'social reproduction' and voluntary work, particularly work done by women?

In other words, if the aim is to ensure that as many people as possible are integrated into the labour market, we should be careful not to define that concept too narrowly; we should incorporate it into some overall, culture-based, thinking about social well-being.

Consequently, work and the demand for it from an increasing number of people should be taken seriously, while less importance should be attached to the forms it currently takes as these are tied to a partially outdated cultural framework.

In economic and work terms, these studies show that Europe needs to take a pragmatic and realistic approach. It must start giving some deliberate, forward-looking thought to the matter, as part of its plans for tomorrow's society – with due regard at all times, of course, for the diversity of cultures and employment systems which are one of Europe's assets and might yet work to its advantage in the future.

Chapter 3

Summaries of the studies

- *Technological and economic questions associated with the future of work*
  Summary of the study carried out by François Beaujolin
- *Sociological literature on the future of work*
  Summary of the study carried out by Pertti Koistinen and Ari Nieminen
- *Regulating work and welfare in the future:*
  Towards a new social contract or a new gender contract?
  Summary of the study carried out by Jacqueline O'Reilly and Claudia Spee
- *The emergence of new forms of professional conduct and new structures of work in local development and employment initiatives*
  Summary of the study conducted by Isabelle Perguilhem and Laurent Gardin with the assistance of Jacques Gautrat, Centre de recherche et d'information sur la démocratie et l'autonomie – CRIDA– with the assistance of the Laboratoire de sociologie du changement des institutions – LSCI/CNRS (French National Research Centre)

3.1. TECHNOLOGICAL AND ECONOMIC QUESTIONS ASSOCIATED WITH THE FUTURE OF WORK

Summary of the study carried out by François Beaujolin[43]

In the light of economic and technological changes, two contrasting views of work conditions in the years to come emerge from the international literature on the future of work: there may be a shortage of work in industrialized countries, either because of unfair competition from newly industrialized countries or because automation will replace manpower. Work will change in response to new technology, but also as a result of organizational choices, changes in demand and differential gains in productivity, shifting boundaries between organizations and new modes of co-operation in organizations.

By analysing these two views, we can find answers to these two very different crises affecting work: a possible shortage of work gives rise to job-sharing, a severing of the link between work and income and a lowering of the cost of work; changes in work and the qualifications required raise questions about working for a regular salary, increasing job insecurity, flexibility, mobility, initial training, continuing training, ageing, and so on.

3.1.1. Is there no future for work any more?

Debate 1: Globalization, a cause of unemployment in developed countries

All Northern countries are, to a greater or lesser extent, addressing the question of 'social dumping' by the newly industrialized countries. In the United States and in France, the debate is particularly lively. One theory crops up frequently: globalization

---

[43] François Beaujolin is a consultant for GESTE – Groupe d'Etudes Sociales Techniques et Sociales – Paris.

will lead to large-scale job-destruction in the developed countries. After the traditional industries, which were first in the firing line, relocation is now affecting technological products, services, agriculture and the agri-food industry. While it may be impossible to measure, the link between unemployment and relocation cannot be denied. These gloomy analyses have been criticized by American and European scholars. Most American studies conclude that salary trends in countries like the US, the UK, Japan and France are due to factors other than changes affecting the structure of trade. The French approach is more comprehensive: it takes account of the offset in exports of skilled-labour-intensive goods, the offset in exports of capital and intermediate goods arising from the additional purchasing power of the exporting countries, and the setting up of French firms abroad.

There now seems to be consensus on two conclusions: firstly, the impact is greater than was originally thought because it is highly concentrated in particular industries and, secondly, where the industrialized countries are concerned, economies of scale have had a lot to do with the substantial gains in productivity brought about by trade. The main conclusion of these studies is that most manufacturing industry in industrialized countries is now in industries which rely heavily on skilled workers and innovation and which are not directly threatened with relocation to low-wage countries.

Debate 2: Technological unemployment in the third industrial revolution

The drive to substitute capital for labour has always brought with it the question of the 'end of work'. The challenge in the current debate is to show that, before the 'knowledge revolution', overspill (from primary to secondary, and then from secondary to tertiary), lessened the impact of the capital/labour substitution, but that the circumstances of this technological revolution are radically new and therefore require radical responses.

47

The End of Work, a book by the American Marxist J. Rifkin, starts with a description of the characteristics of the 'end of work' as they are currently perceived: intelligent machines replace human beings in most tasks. This industrial revolution is different from the others in that it does not generate a new economic sector that can absorb the millions of newly-unemployed people. The 'end of work' is a phenomenon that affects the whole world and crosses sectoral lines.

Criticism is levelled at this belief in the dawning of a new age from four different angles:

- some would dispute that productivity is rising again – consider R.M. Solow's productivity paradox: 'computers are everywhere, except in productivity statistics';
- not everyone subscribes to the philosophy of growth – this argument postulates that household requirements for goods and services are finite, ultimately satiable, which puts a limit on viable production at any given time. But most economists are opposed to this theory, some of them vigorously so;
- the overspill crisis needs to be seen in context;
- there are question marks over the proposed solutions.

Debate 3: The unemployment rate decreases as the level of training increases

It is widely recognized, in all countries, that the unemployed are less well-educated than people with jobs, that many unemployed people have a low level of education and that the unemployment rate is higher among low-skilled workers. However, the causes of this state of affairs are less well understood. Is it competition? Not enough skills to meet the demands of technological progress? The wages paid to low-skilled workers? The mismatch between the output from initial training courses and the manpower needs of the economy? The way recruitment is being managed by employers?

The theory of skewed technological progress – which discriminates against unskilled workers – is a relatively new one (it appeared at the beginning of the 1990s, particularly in the United States). The traditional image of technical progress was more or less that it 'de-skilled' people. However, many specialists now believe that information technology changes the nature of technological progress. The new forms of technology complement skilled work and can replace unskilled work. The authors of the European studies consider that the evidence for skewed technological progress is rather limited and indirect.

Others dispute the theory of skewed technological progress and put forward various alternative explanations. Advances in software may make the distinction between skilled and unskilled work less clear-cut. The fact that people with certain skills are 'overpaid' at the moment will encourage other workers to obtain the qualifications needed to join the occupations concerned. The skills needed to use the new forms of technology do not necessarily invalidate the skills possessed by workers who are poorly qualified. The important thing, therefore, is to identify teaching methods that would enable workers regarded as unskilled to obtain the new qualifications they need in a short space of time. Any potential solution would also have to take account of a second factor: organizational changes and their impact on the skills needed in a work situation.

Are the wages paid to low-skilled workers too high?

When we correlate the effects of changes in the minimum wage on employment levels with the impact of the minimum wage on unemployment, the findings are far from unequivocal. The debate is a complex and contradictory one.

In view of the paradoxical results from studies in OECD member countries, the OECD has become more cautious in drawing conclusions in recent years. In 1996, the OECD admitted that it was difficult to tell whether the minimum wage, which limits the number of poorly paid jobs, also has a negative effect on the overall chances of low-skilled and inexperienced workers finding a job. The most recent OECD study concludes that the greater pay inequality, its causes and consequences will probably be studied and hotly debated for a long time to come.

Does initial training produce over-qualification?

Alongside the 'human capital' and 'credentialist' schools, a theory has developed that there is a 'mismatch' between initial education and employment. This approach focuses on the conflicts that arise because the educational and productive systems operate quite independently of each other.

In 1996, L. Mallet co-ordinated the work of six European research teams on competition for jobs through ability rather than qualifications. The conclusion was that there was no shortage of ability in the market: demand is not nearly as important as supply in explaining the changes in skill structures. The conclusions concerning demand for qualifications by employers were that the effects of technological progress, which work to the advantage of bright candidates, were at their most marked in the 1960s, but waned considerably in the 1970s and, once again, in the 1980s. Despite the drastic industrial restructuring of the 1980s, the effects on professions requiring intellectual ability fell to their lowest point during that period. The second conclusion is that there is a disparity between the growth in demand for intellectual skills and their supply. The American educational system produces a much higher number of educated workers than the labour market can absorb. This type of study also illustrates the vast dissimilarities between the situations of low-skilled workers in different countries.

Do companies' human-resource policies exclude low-skilled workers?

The assumption is that employers respond to the growth in the supply of skilled workers by raising their requirements, not because they necessarily need better qualified workers to carry out the work, but because they recruit the best candidates available. This research shows that the first two assumptions (technological bias and minimum wage level) are always a bone of contention, while the other two (different rates of growth in the supply of and demand for qualifications, together with recruitment of overqualified workers) are generally not in dispute.

Answers to the 'end of work'

Two solutions have been put forward by the proponents of one of the theories on the 'end of work' for some or all workers (globalization and/or relocation + unemployment on technological grounds): one involves job-sharing, the other a cut in payroll costs for low-skilled workers.

1) Can work be shared?

As the amount of work available has decreased, the idea of 'job-sharing' has gained currency everywhere. The idea that there is a long-term trend towards shorter working hours has come under attack from two angles: firstly, it is said that reductions occur only at irregular intervals and, secondly, some countries seem to have gone through a more complex pattern of historical development. The idea of widespread and compulsory job-sharing has been criticized, often savagely, as 'utopian, naive and dangerous – not worthy of serious consideration'.

In the light of the experiments run in various European countries in the 1980s, the literature suggests some principles to govern the reduction of working time which provide some scope for risk-taking:

- implementation of the scheme and hence negotiations between employers and workers should be decentralized;
- there should be partial (i.e. neither full nor zero) compensation to offset salary loss;

51

- there should be neutral arrangements for social security contributions depending on the length of working time chosen (to benefit part-time workers);
- the measure, in a 'defensive' context (as part of a social plan), is one of the least costly to subsidize of the various employment policy instruments.

In European countries that do not use the reduction or adjustment of working hours as a weapon against unemployment, the calmness of the debate suggests that such a policy is pursued as a social good in itself.

2) What effects are lower labour costs for low-skilled workers expected to have?

Globalization may pose a problem in terms of the level of wages paid to low-skilled workers in the developed countries. However, because of the wage gap, lowering the cost of work is not seen as an appropriate response to the challenges created by international trade. Strategic positioning of companies and countries, together with partial or temporary social safety measures, seems like the only answer.

The two-fold objective behind reducing working time is: to cut down on the substitution of capital for labour and to make unskilled labour more attractive by comparison with skilled labour.

Conclusion: End of work or endless qualifications?

Following this first round of discussions on the possibility of a new crisis for mankind, recent studies offer some more detailed insights that show that there is a considerable degree of consensus:

- globalization has undoubtedly had an effect on low-skilled workers, but the rate of job losses has probably levelled off now;

- productivity gains do not cause unemployment if the social, cultural and financial conditions are right for overspill towards activities involving inter-relating;
- the difficulties faced by low-skilled workers are probably due more to the demand effect (raising the level of qualifications amongst the active population) than the supply effect (the need for skilled workers for technological reasons);
- the fall in the cost of work (through the lowering of employers' social security contributions) could – with the correct refinancing – result in new jobs for low-skilled workers;
- cutting working hours is probably not the ideal way of combating unemployment, even though we now have a better idea of how to make it work.

The thread that runs through all these areas is the problem of qualifications: the jobs of the future will probably be less conceptual and require more inter-relating skills (increase in third-sector jobs). Reductions in working hours make versatility and multifunctionality all the more important. Information technology requires different skills from the technology of the industrial revolution. The shifting of added value in the developed countries towards 'advanced' design and production tasks requires constant reskilling.

The key to all the issues considered here appears to be speed of adjustment to the massive conversion of manpower skills required in developed countries.

3.1.2. Work is changing

The causes of the current organizational changes

Technological change is perhaps not the main cause of unemployment, but it has paved the way for substantial changes in the organization of work and consequent increases in productivity. The changeover from a market-oriented economic phase dominated by supply to one where the market is based on the renewal of previous stock reverses the relationship between supply and demand and gives the customer the upper hand.

There are two concerns: finding the conditions for internationally recognized quality production and a diverse supply of products for niche markets (variety) which are neglected by mass production. The organizational principles of the economy of variety preceded the use of suitable decentralized information tools. The partial devolution of the decision-making power to the units nearest to the information (an organizational principle that makes for a rapid reaction) is bolstered by the development of bigger and busier communications networks. Although the flexible production model does not yet have a well-established theoretical basis, this will probably be expanded in the coming decades.

Recasting the boundaries between organizations and rethinking salaried work

The first consequence of the new technical and organizational production model is that it creates the need for a rethink about the traditional boundaries between organizations and, more generally, the forms which employment takes. The impact on human-resource management in businesses is very marked:

- *The network company:* the economic dynamics of international competition, aided by advances in communication, have produced semi-integrated companies that do business with others and cluster into groups resembling nebulae or solar systems. The defining characteristic of these configurations is that they form a structure containing companies which are independent of each other in terms of capital within a single value chain.
- *Increasing insecurity in the job market:* as we mourn the demise of salaried work, the future of work belongs to the self-employed worker. Two theories, one American (Bridges) and

one French (Morin) differ on the role of management. Bridges thinks there is no need for managers any longer, because workers no longer need to be managed. In Morin's view, however, micro-management (direct, close-up supervision) of resources and the human constraints which will arise from this system will become highly developed.

- *Teleworking:* a new way of doing old work, has been a hotly debated topic. Attempts to make a quantitative assessment of it have been particularly controversial since no widely accepted definition has yet been arrived at. Several complementary ideas have emerged from the work on the major amendments to labour law required by the changes in work itself: professionalization and increased autonomy, breakdown of the work contract, working time and individualization, and changes in the sources of law.

All of these developments lead towards the disappearance of the notion of collective identity and place emphasis on the individual identity of the paid worker. The 'professionalization' of work makes the growth in autonomy and the loss of collective identity more marked. The 'skills' rationale has had an effect on the development of labour law: a gradual dilution of the concept of subordination and the right to a professional qualification.

The breakdown of the work contract

Two factors have been leading to the breakdown of the traditional work contract. Firstly, the focus on specialization has led to the replacement of the work contract by commercial contracts between large firms and their networks of subcontractors. Secondly, government policies on social integration through work, as part of the battle against unemployment, weaken the collective identity of workers by fostering the development of 'atypical' work.

- *The future of wage earners:* several authors refer to organizational recoil forces. The boundaries between organizations are certainly changing and firms are probably focusing more on their core activities. Yet the new organizational landscape of inter-company co-operation does seem to be following rules. There is some resistance to the disappearance of organizations in that outsourcing is not just an economic choice between 'doing' and 'buying', but means abandoning certain skills. It seems that new, relatively stable organizational forms are coming into being. The reshaping of the economic fabric around contractors and first-level subcontractors, or new companies providing services to private individuals and firms, may compensate for the clear reduction in the capacity for integration through the classic route of salaried work in a large industrial company. Yet there still seems to be a future for wage-earning. The current literature suggests that the salaried society should continue to exist, at different levels, even if the trend is towards individuals having greater control over their own work and their professional future.
- *Working time is becoming increasingly individualized:* the idea of 'collective' labour law is under particular threat when it comes to working time. The disappearance of a collective work identity and its replacement by a more individual identity have certain implications for the future, as regards:
  - a shrinking of the socially integrating function of work;
  - a tendency for the distinction between salaried workers and the self-employed to become more fluid;
  - an identity and protection for the unskilled;
  - the forms of collective representation and organization.

New forms of co-ordination within organizations

In the quest for new forms of organization that meet the various challenges posed by the production of goods and services, three are described in detail: concurrent project management, horizontal co-operation and vertical stratification. Their common feature is co-operation between players in the organization, and they are designed to respond to the needs of 'flexible production'. These three forms are not mutually exclusive: each new organization combines them, leaning towards the 'permissive bureaucracy' which is still to be established.

This new production model, still at the gestation stage, forms the basis for proposals for organizational models: P. Zarifian's 'skill-building organization' and P. Adler's 'enabling bureaucracy'. Two series of social consequences are identified in the literature: the rise of the tertiary sector (the intensification of symbolic activities and social interaction brought about by the production processes puts work itself in the tertiary sector, not just jobs) and the identification of the knowledge needed in these organizations.

Lifelong learning is certainly one recommendation that would help us to cope with the permanent organizational precariousness caused by this new flexible-production model.

Regarding the mobilization of knowledge, there are several studies from various sources which attempt to define the areas of knowledge required by the new organizations. These new ways of looking at the problem of mobilising knowledge in a work framework have shed new light on where knowledge is acquired ('sit-down training' and 'stand-up training') and on the disqualification of the lowest category of unskilled wage-earners.

Putting into perspective some of the human-resource management issues that stem from the sweeping changes to work

Skills-acquisition by workers is obviously an important issue: organizational revolutions, whether they involve rethinking the boundaries between organizations or developing new forms of co-ordination in organizations, bring problems with skills, qualifications and training in their wake. Research into industrial districts in France and particularly Italy, reveals the importance of largely informal, local intermeshing for economic strength and a dynamic labour market. This emerging awareness of the importance of the local dimension in employment management has given rise to debates, proposals and applications which highlight the legal, social, political and other difficulties to be surmounted if the new challenges are to be met. Several initiatives involving the structuring of the labour market in specific areas have been given support over recent years: local plans for integrating people into working life through the economy, multi-annual arrangements and employers' groupings.

3.1.3. Bibliography

Adler, P. (1992), *Technology and the future of work,* Oxford University Press, New York and Oxford.

Adler, P. (1993), The learning bureaucracy: NUMMI; in: Staw, Barry M., Cummings, Larry L. (eds.) *Research in organizational behavior,* Vol. 15, 1993, Greenwich, CT: JAI Press.

Adler, P., Borys, B. (1996), Two types of bureaucracy: Enabling and coercitive; in: *Administrative Science Quarterly,* Vol. 41.

Adler, P., Cole, R. (1993), Designed for learning: A tale of two auto plans; in: *Sloan Management Review,* spring 1993.

Alasoini, T. (1996), The Finnish national workplace development programme, Working papers 3, Ministry of labour, Helsinki.

Alter, N., Laville, J.-L., Linhart, D., Maurice, M., Segrestin, D., Veltz, P., Zarifian, P. (1993), Systèmes productifs: les modèles en question; in: *Sociologie du travail* (special issue 35), 1/1993.

ANACT (Agence Nationale pour l'Amélioration des Conditions de Travail) (1991), *La requalification d'ouvriers de faible niveau: le cas d'une usine automobile,* Coll. Points de Repères, Éd. ANACT.

Aoki, M., Gustafsson, B. Williamson, O. (1990), *The firm as a nexus of treaties,* Sage Publications, London.

Aronsson, G., Leijon, A.-G. (1994), Samh ällsomvandling och arbetsliv. Omv ärldsanalys infor 2000-talet, Solna, Arbetmiljöininstitutet.

Arthuis, J. (1993), *Les délocalisations et l'emploi,* Les Editions d'Organisation, Paris.

Baldwin, R. (1994), Les effets des échanges et de l'investissement direct international sur l'emploi et les salaires relatifs; in: *Revue économique de l'OCDE,* No 23, Winter 1994.

Barbier, J.-C., Nadel, H. (1996), L'évolution des systèmes de protection sociale en Europe. Crises des Etats providence et reconfiguration; in: *Revue Française des Affaires Sociales,* January–March 1996.

Barbier, J.-M., Berton, F., Boru, J.-J. (1996), *Situations de travail et formation,* L'Harmattan, Coll. Action et Savoir, Paris.

Bardelli, P. (1996), *Le modèle de production flexible,* PUF, Paris.

Baudry, B. (1995), *L'économie des relations interentreprises,* Repères, La Découverte, Paris.

Belasco, J., Stayer, R. (1994), Why empowerment doesn't empower: The bankruptcy of current paradigms; in: *Business Horizons,* March–April 1994.

Bérard, D. (1996), *Télétravail et nouvelles formes d'organisation du travail,* ANACT, Lyon.

Berggren, C. (1992), *Alternatives to lean production: Work organisation in the Swedish auto industry,* IRL Press, Ithaca, New York.

Blanc, G. (éd.) (1995), *Le travail au XXIème siècle. Mutations de l'économie et de la société à l'ère des autoroutes de l'information,* Dunod, Paris.

Blasco, P., Loubet, D. (1995), *Le télétravail,* Éd. d'Organisation, Paris.

Boissonnat, J., Mabit, R. (1995), *Le travail dans 20 ans,* Éd. Odile Jacob – La Documentation Française, Paris.

Boskin, M., Dulberger, E., Griliches, Z., Gordon, R., Jorgensen, D. (1996), Toward a more accurate measure of the cost of living, Final report to the Senate Finance Committee, December, USA.

Breton, T. (1994), Le télétravail en France, Coll. rapports officiels, La Documentation Française, Paris.

Bridges, W. (1994), *Jobshift,* Addison-Wesley, Reading, Mass. trad. française (1995), *La conquête du travail,* Éd.Village mondial, Paris.

Brilman, J. (1996), *L'entreprise réinventée,* Éd. d'Organisation, Paris.

Brousseau, E. (1993), L'économie des contrats. Technologies de l'information et co-ordination d'entreprises; in: *Economie en liberté,* P.U.F, Paris.

Brunhes, B. (1996), *Les habits neufs de l'emploi,* MIL-édition, Paris.

Calvez, J.-Y. (1997), *Nécessité du travail: disparition d'une valeur ou redéfinition,* Éd. de l'Atelier, Paris.

Caracuel, M.-R. (1992), Formas de reordenación y reducción del tiempo de trabajo, *Revista de economía y sociológica del trabajo,* No 15–16/1992.

Cases, C., Saunier, J.-M., Volovitch, P. (1996), Le financement de la protection sociale en Europe; in:, *Solidarité santé* – Etudes statistiques, January–March 1996.

Castel, R. (1995), Le salariat est plus qu'un héritage de l'histoire; in: *Economie et Humanisme,* No 334, October 1995.

Centre Info its magazine *Education permanente.*

CEREQ (Centre d'Etude et de Recherche sur l'Emploi et les Qualifications) its magazine *Education et emploi.*

Cette, G., Cuneo, P., Eyssartier, D., Gautié, J. (1995), Les effets sur l'emploi d'un abaissement du coût du travail des jeunes: quelques éléments d'évaluation, dans Benhayoun, G., Bazen, S., *Salaire minimum et bas salaires,* L'Harmattan, Paris.

CGP (Commissariat Général du Plan) (1995), *Le travail dans 20 ans,* Éd. Odile Jacob, Paris.

CNAM (Conservatoire National des Arts et Métiers) and its training units for adults and trainers.

Cohen, D. (1997), *Richesse du monde, pauvreté des nations,* Essais, Flamarion, Paris.

Cohen, E. (1996), *La tentation hexagonale. La souveraineté à l'épreuve de la mondialisation,* Fayard, Paris.

Coriat, B. (1990), *L'atelier et le robot,* et (1991), *Penser à l'envers,* Bourgois, Paris.

Corneo, G. (1995), Ajustement des cotisations sociales et chômage d'équilibre; in: *Economie et Prévision*, No 115, 1995–4.

Cortes, O., Sébastien, J. (1997), Les échanges internationaux modifient la demande de travail; in: *Economie et Statistique*, No 301–302, 1997–1/2.

Cotis, J.-P., Germain, J.-M., Quinet, A. (1997), Les effets du progrès technique sur le travail peu qualifiés sont indirects et limités; in: *Economie et Statistique*, No 301–302, 1997–1/2.

CSERC (Centre Supérieur de l'Emploi, des Revenus et des Coûts) (1996), *L'allégement des charges sociales sur les bas salaires,* La Documentation Française, Paris.

Davies, A., Nashold, F., Pritchard, W., Reve, T. (1993), *Evaluation report*, Commissioned by the board of the Norwegian SBA Programme.

de Foucauld, J.-B. (1995), *Le financement de la protection sociale,* La Documentation Française, Paris.

de Terssac, G., Dubois, P. (**éd**) (1992), *Les nouvelles rationalisations de la production,* CEPADUES, Toulouse.

de Virville, M. (1996), *Donner un nouvel élan à la formation professionnelle,* La Documentation Française.

Debonneuil, M., Lahidji, R. (1995), Le chômage en France: une occasion pour changer de société; in: *Scénarios pour l'emploi,* Economica, Paris.

Dolata, U. (1997), *Das Phantom der Globalisierung*, Blätter für deutsche und internationale Politik, 1997–1.

Dormont, B., Pauchet, M. (1997), L'élasticité de l'emploi au coût salarial dépend-elle des structures de qualification? In: *Economie et Statistique*, No 301–302, 1997–1/2.

DREE-Résultats, Many articles since 1993.

Drèze, J., Sneessens, H. (1995), Progrès technique, mondialisation et travail peu qualifié; in: *Scénarios pour l'emploi*, Economica, Paris.

Drèze, J., Sneessens, H. (1995), Progrès technique, mondialisation et travail peu qualifié; in: *Pour l'emploi, la croissance et l'Europe,* (ed). De Boeck Université, Bruxelles.

Durand, J.-P. (1993), *Vers un nouveau système productif,* Syros, Paris.

Economie et Statistique (Revue) (1997), Several special issues about the career paths of young people. No 273, 1994–3, No 283–284, 1995–3/4, No 304–305, 1997–4/5.

Euzéby, A. (1996), Les impôts et le financement de la Protection Sociale; in: *Les cahiers français,* No 274, 2ᵉ trimestre.

Everaere, C. (1997), *Management de la flexibilité,* Coll. Gestion, Economica, Paris.

Fitoussi, J.-P. (1995), Les figures du possible et de l'utopique; in: *Scénarios pour l'emploi,* Economica, Paris.

Fitoussi, J.-P., Luna, F. (1996), Wage distribution, social cohesion and the knowledge-based economy; in: *Employment and growth in the knowledge-based economy,* OECD Documents, Paris.

Fitoussi, J.-P., Rosanvallon, P. (1996), *Le nouvel âge des inégalités,* Coll. Essais, Le Seuil, Paris.

Fixari, D., Moisdon, J.-C., Weil, B. (1996), Former pour transformer: la longue marche des actions de requalification; in: *Cahiers de Recherche,* No 10, CGS, Ecole des Mines de PARIS.

Forrester, V. (1996), *L'horreur économique,* Fayard, Paris.

Franck, B., Maroy, C. (1996), *Formation et socialisation au travail,* De Boeck, coll. Perspectives en éducation. This collective work was published after the 1994 Leuven Symposium of the International Network of Research on Life-Long Learning.

Franzmeyer, F., Lindlar, L., Trabold, H. (1996), *Employment and social policies under international constrains,* Deutsches Institut für Wirtschaftsforschung, Berlin.

Freeman, C. (1995), Le nouveau contexte de l'innovation; in: *STI revue,* No 15.

Fréry, F. (1996), L'entreprise transactionnelle; in: *Gérer et Comprendre,* No 45, September.

Garvin, D. (1993), Building a learning organization; in: *Harvard Business Review,* July–August.

Germain, Jean-Marc., Dormont, Brigitte., Legendre, François et Lemaître, Patricia., Mihoubi, Ferhat., Dormont,

Brigitte et Pauchet, Marianne (1997), Five articles on the labour cost; in: *Economie et Statistique,* INSEE Newsletter (No 301–302), 1997–1/2.

Giard, V., Midler, C. (direction), **ECOSIP** (1993), *Pilotages de projet et entreprises. Diversités et convergences,* Coll. Gestion, Economica, Paris.

Ginsbourger, F., Merle, V., Vergnaud, G. (1992), *Formation et apprentissage des adultes peu qualifiés,* La Documentation Française, Paris.

Granier, P., Michel, P. (1995), Les conflits d'intérêt entre travailleurs qualifiés et travailleurs non qualifiés; in: *Economie et Prévision,* No 115, 1995–4.

Greenan, N., Guellec, D. (1994), Organisation du travail, technologie et performances: une étude empirique; in: *Economie et Prévision,* No 113–114, 2–3/1994.

Greenan, N. (1996), Innovation technologique, changements organisationnels et évolution des compétences. Une étude empirique sur l'industrie manufacturière en France; in: *Economie et Statistique,* No 298, 1996–8.

Greenan, N. (1996), Progrès technique et changements organisationnels: leur impact sur l'emploi et les qualifications; in: *Economie et Statistique,* No 298, 1996–8.

Gustavsen, B., Hofmaier, B., Ekman, M., Philips, M., Wikman, A. (1995), *Utveckslinjer i arbetslivet och arbetslivsfondets roll,* SNS, Stockholm.

Hall, R. (1987), *Attaining manufacturing excellence,* Dow Jones – Irwin, Homewood, Illinois.

Hamermesh, D. (1993), *Labor Demand,* Princeton University Press.

Hatchuel, A., Weil, B. (1992), *L'expert et le système, Quatre histoires de systèmes-experts,* Economica, Paris.

Houben, H., Ingham, M. (1995), Par quel système remplacer le fordisme? In: *Gérer et Comprendre,* December.

Imai, M. (1989), *Kaïzen. La clé de la compétitivité japonaise,* Eyrolles, Paris.

63

Jarillo, J.-C. (1993), *Strategic networks. Creating the borderless organization,* Butterworth-Heinemann, Oxford.

Kasvio, A. (1994), *Uusi työn yhteiskunta. Suomalaisen työlään muutokset ja kehittämismahdollisuudet.* Gaudeamus, Helsinki.

Kern, H., Schumann, M. (1984), *Das ende der Arbeitsteilung,* Beck, München, French version (1989), *La fin de la division du travail,* Maison des Sciences de l'Homme, Paris.

Larruturou, P. (1994), *Ca ne peut plus durer,* Le Seuil, Paris.

Lave, J., Wenger, E. (1991), *Situated learning: Legitimate peripherical participation,* Cambridge University Press, Cambridge.

Laville, J.-L. (1994), Services, emploi et socialisation; in: *Cohésion sociale et emploi,* Desclée de Brouver, Paris.

Lee, E. (1996), La mondialisation et l'emploi: des craintes justifiées? In: *Revue Internationale du Travail,* No 5.

Lehndorf, S. (1995), La redistribution de l'emploi en Allemagne; in: *Futuribles,* No 195, February, Paris.

Lemesle, R. M., Marot, J. C. (1996), *Le télétravail,* P.U.F, Paris.

Lequiller, F. (1997), L'indice des prix à la consommation surestime-t-il l'inflation? In: *Economie et Statistique,* No 303, 1997–3.

Lesourne, J. (1997), Penser la société d'information; in: *Réseaux,* January-February.

Lesourne, J. (1997), *Vérités et mensonges sur le chômage,* Coll. Opus, Éd. Odile Jacob, Paris.

LIRHE (Laboratoire Interdisciplinaire de Recherches sur l'Emploi et les Ressources Humaines, headed by Louis Mallet, Toulouse) (coordination) et CEDEFOP (finance) (1996), Rapport de synthèse d'une étude comparative menée en Allemagne, Espagne, France, Italie, Pays-Bas, Royaume-Uni, October.

Lundvall, B., Johnson, B. (1994), The learning economy; in: *Journal of Industry Studies,* Vol. I, No 2.

Lundvall, B.-X. (ed.) (1992), *National systems of innovation: Towards a theory on innovation and interactive learning,* Pinter, London.

Lynch, L.M. (ed.) (1994), *Training and the private sector: International comparisons,* University of Chicago Press, Chicago.

Maillard, D. (1995), Financement de la protection sociale: quel est le problème? In: *Chroniques Economiques – SEDEIS*, No 9, September.

Malglaive, G. (1990), *Enseigner à des adultes*, P.U.F, Paris.

Mathieu, C., Sterdyniak, H. (1994), L'émergence de l'Asie en développement menace-t-elle l'emploi en France? In: *Observations et diagnostics économiques – Revue de l'OFCE*, January.

Méda, D. (1995), *Le travail, une valeur en voie de disparition*, Alto – Aubier, Paris.

Méda, D. (1996), Travail, emploi, activité: de quoi parle-t-on? In: *Données Sociales*, INSEE, Paris.

Méda, D. (1997), *La littérature américaine sur le travail. Un aperçu à travers trois livres récents*, mimeo.

Micelli, S.(1995), NUMMI versus Uddevalla: apprentissage et mémoire dans la production industrielle; in: *Sociologie du travail*, No 3/95.

Middleton, J., Ziderman, A., van Adams, A. (1993), *Skills for productivity: Vocational education and training in developing countries*, Oxford University Press, Oxford.

Mills, D. (French version 1994), *L'entreprise post-hiérarchique*, Inter-éditions, Paris.

Ministère du Travail (1996), Les groupements d'employeurs. Evaluation dans le cadre de la loi quinquennale. Non-published report.

Mintzberg, H. (1981), *The structuring of organizations:A synthesis of the research*, Prentice-Hall, New York, trad. française (1984), *Structure et dynamique des organisations*, Éd. Organisation, Paris.

MIRE (*1995 and 1996*), *Comparer les systèmes de protection sociale en Europe.*

Moati, P. (1996), Division cognitive du travail et dynamique de la localisation industrielle dans l'espace mondial; in: *Cahier de recherche*, No 89, June 96, CREDOC (Centre de Recherche pour l'Etude et l'Observation des Conditions de vie), Paris.

Molet, H. (1993), *Une nouvelle gestion industrielle*, Hermès, Paris.

Morin, P. (1994), *La grande mutation du travail et de l'emploi. Emploi juste-à-temps et travail éclaté dans la société postindustrielle,* Éd. d'Organisation, Paris.

Naschold, F. (ed.) (1993), *Constructing the new industrial society,* Van Gorcum & Swedish centre for working life, Assen & Stockholm.

Nieminen, A. (1997), Labour market regulation and industrial relations in three Nordic countries, working paper, Universities of Helsinki & Tampere.

OECD (1994), *L'étude sur l'emploi. Données et explications,* OECD, Paris.

OECD (1994), *L'étude de l'OCDE sur l'emploi. Données et explications,* OECD.

OECD (July 1996), *Employment outlook,* OECD, Paris.

OECD (January 1996), *Le système espagnol de sécurité sociale: évolution et perspectives,* Etudes Economiques.

OECD (1996), *Perspectives de la science, de la technologie et de l'industrie,* OECD, Paris.

OECD (1996), Technologie, productivité et création d'emplois; in: *Rapport analytique,* Vol. 2, OECD, Paris.

OFCE (Observatoire Français des Conjonctures Economiques) (1996), Coût du travail et emploi des jeunes, report commissioned by the French Senate, Paris.

Ohno, T. (1989), *L'esprit Toyota,* Masson, Paris.

Pailhous, J., Vergnaud, G. (1989), *Adultes en reconversion,* La Documentation Française, Paris.

Pallier, B., Bonoli, G. (1995), Entre Bismark et Beveridge. 'Crises' de la Sécurité Sociale et politique(s); in: *Revue française de sciences politiques,* August.

Pekkola, J., Ylöstalo, P. (1996), *Tietotyö ja työmarkkina-asema.* Työpoliittinen tutkimus, No 158, Työministeriö, Finland.

Perret, B., Roustang, G. (1993), *L'économie contre la société,* Esprit, Le Seuil, Paris.

Porter, M. (1990, trad. française 1994), *L'avantage concurrentiel des nations,* Interéditions, Paris.

Qvortrup, L. (1991), *Telework: Visions, definitions, realities, barriers,* OECD, URBA 2000, Handbook on cities and new technologies, Paris.

Reich, R. (1991), *The work of nations,* Vintage Book, New York, French version (1993), *L'économie mondialisée,* Dunod, Paris.

Rifkin, J. (1995), *The end of work: The decline of the labor force and the dawn of the post-market era,* G. P. Putman's Sons, New York.

Rigaudiat, J. (1993), *Réduire le temps de travail,* Syros, Paris.

Rossi, M., Sartori, E. (1995), *Ripensare la solidarietà,* Locarno, Armando Dado.

Rozenholc, A., Fanton, B., Veyret, A. (1995), *Téléemploi, télééconomie. Une chance pour l'emploi et l'attractivité des territoires,* IDATE, DATAR, Paris.

Ruesga, S. (1995), *La España laboral en la encrucijada,* Anuario de Economía, Madrid.

Saralegui, J.-B. (1995), *Reparto del tiempo de trabajo como medida de creación de empleo. El caso vasco,* Ekonomiaz, No 31–32.

Schmidt, G., O'Reilly, J., Schömann, K. (1996), *International Handbook of Labour market policy and Evaluation,* Edward Elgar, Cheltenham.

Schwartz, B. (1994), *Moderniser sans exclure,* La Découverte, Coll. Essais.

Serieyx, H. (1996), Les incidences des changements d'organisation des entreprises sur la nature et l'organisation du travail et de l'emploi en France, étude de la section Travail du Conseil Economique et Social, Paris.

Serrano, C. (1996), Los efectos visibles de la reforma laboral de 1994; in: *Cuadernos de información económica,* March.

Shingo (1987), *Le système SMED. Une révolution en gestion de production,* Éd. d'Organisation, Paris.

Shor, J. (1995), *The overworked American, the unexpected decline of leisure,* Basic Book.

Solow, R. (1995), Problèmes et perspectives de la croissance économique; in: *Scénarios pour l'emploi,* Economica, Paris.

Stern, D. (1996), Human resource development in the knowledge-based economy; in: *Employment and growth knowledge-based economy,* OECD documents.

Supiot, A. (1994), *Critique du droit du travail,* Les voies du droit, Presses Universitaires de France, Paris.

Vimont, C. (1993), *Le commerce extérieur français: créateur ou destructeur d'emplois?,* Economica, Paris.

Wolff, E. (1996), Technologie et demande de qualifications; in: *Revue Science Technologie Industrie (STI),* No 18, OCDE.

Womack, J.-P., Jones, D.T., Roos, D. (1990), *The machine that changed the world,* Macmillan, New York, French version (1992), *Le système qui va changer le monde,* Dunod, Paris.

Wood, A. (1995), How trade hurt unskilled workers; in: *Journal of Economic Perspectives,* summer, Vol. 9, No 3.

Zarifian, P. (1993), *Quels modèles d'organisation pour l'industrie européenne,* L'Harmattan, Paris.

Zimmermann, K.F. (1995), Wage and mobility effects of trade and migration, quoted by Olivier Cortès et Jean Sébastien; in: *Economie et Statistique,* No 301–302, 1997–1/2.

Zürn, M. (1996), Zum Verhältnis von Globalisierung, politischer Integration und politischer Fragmentierung; in: *Fricke W.* (Hrsg.).

3.2. SOCIOLOGICAL LITERATURE ON THE FUTURE OF WORK

Summary of the study carried out by Pertti Koistinen & Ari Nieminen[44]

3.2.1. Work in modern society

Theorising on work and society during the 1990s

The sociological concepts of 'the crisis of paid work', 'the end of work' and 'the two-thirds society' have been attracting interest and have been given various interpretations since the 1960s and 1970s. But the recession in the 1990s made these theories even more topical.

It was argued that work was becoming less important as a source of individual identity and welfare, and that it was divided unequally among people of working age and unevenly throughout the different stages of an individual's life. A number of factors have led authors to this conclusion:

- the decline in working hours;
- the rise in levels of consumption;
- the division of work between work rich and work poor;
- the changing patterns of work-related social mobility and socialization.

The polarization of working life is leading to the emergence of a two-thirds society (Dahrendorf). According to this theory, we are witnessing the development of a society where two-thirds of the population are in paid employment, with the remaining third excluded from the world of work. There are a number of questions that we need to examine:

---

[44] Both work at the department of social policy of the University of Tampere (Finland).

- The value of work in modern society – how central is it?
- How does work relate to income?
- Who can afford to work less?
- Is society becoming more polarized as new non-class based social divisions emerge?
- Who has the power to choose how they work?
- What is the relationship between salaried work and self-employment, paid work and unpaid work, private-sector employment and public-sector employment?
- How does work relate to training?

Changing functions of work

In a modern society, work – especially paid work – has three functions: production, re-distribution and socialization.

- *Production*: no-one doubts that this is a permanent feature;
- *Distribution*: income trends are increasingly linked to labour productivity, and the requirements and standards it imposes;
- *Socialization*: work has been and seems still to be one of the main arenas for socialization throughout an individual's life.

However, the debate on these functions of salaried work has not always been calm or harmonious; on the contrary, it has been associated with social tension and inequality. Now the traditional forms of work are becoming rare and new forms of work are gaining ground, there is fairly broad agreement that European employment systems and society at large are once again in crisis. There are certain points that require discussion if we are to assess the role of work in society. For instance, is paid work still the most innovative and efficient form of production? Are the new forms of business creation, self-employment and 'social economy' replacing traditional forms of work? Is the fragmentation of work (flexible contracts, self-employment, and so on) giving rise to new social divisions in society? How do unemployment and the scarcity of paid work affect the socialization of those with work? And those without work? All of these changes have an undeniable effect on the role work, particularly paid work, plays in society. Societies are forced to find new and better ways of encouraging their members to take part in production and indeed in society.

3.2.2. Social dimension of work

Social rights and work

In a modern society, social rights are based on citizenship and work. In parallel to the development of universal social rights enjoyed by all citizens, other social rights have been established on the basis of employment contracts, individuals' employment history and employees' own contributions. Rights based on work can be divided into four categories:

- democratic rights at work;
- the right to training and well-being;
- contractual rights;
- social security rights.

All these highly developed social rights are linked to wage labour. After all the transformations that working life has undergone, there are a number of basic questions to be answered. Does the fragmentation of work (flexible contracts, self-employment, and so on) give rise to new social divisions in the society? Can paid work continue to be the dominant factor in defining and regulating social rights? Can paid work still serve as the foundation for labour law and regulations or is a new conceptual framework required for labour and social law? These questions seem particularly poignant in Europe because in European history, values such as loyalty, equality, democracy, equal rights for men and women, the quality of life and our relationship, as humans, with nature have taken on a crucial importance. These values have taken root in our individual and collective social memories. And yet there have been changes in people's values and in the way society has developed, changes which force us to re-examine social rights. The growing proportion of women in paid work, the rise in the skill level of the work force, increasingly diverse life-styles and the development of tolerance in multicultural societies are so many new reasons to stress the social dimension.

Social policy in the light of the erosion of the classic employment model

European employers have been moving resolutely towards deregulation. New types of workers have emerged: young workers, women, redundant workers, immigrants, clandestine and black-market labour, illegal home-workers, and so on. This produces new employment relationships, which call for a different type of legal protection, to reflect their various needs and aspirations.

By identifying the so-called 'deviations' from the 'classic' model, we can gauge the efficiency of the protection provided by labour law and collective bargaining. The first deviation is the duration of the contract; the second is the new economic and social relationships, linked to the duration; the third relates to the place where the employee performs the job; the fourth to the triangular relationship between the supplier, the employee, and the user (another firm) for which the employee actually works; and the fifth concerns the content of the worker's obligations. The most sensitive aspect of the employment contract is the worker's provision of his 'physical energies at any given moment'. Multilateral employment relationships have recently sprung up all over the world. These include temporary or interim employment contracts, subcontracting of the workforce, the lending or temporary secondment of workers, and most recently, labour pooling.

Immigrants – A new underclass?

Despite European societies' strong commitment to avoiding social segregation and promoting social integration for immigrant workers and their families, the quest for immigrant labour seems to be a time bomb for Europe. The authors of several studies ask whether European societies are not spawning a new ethnic underclass or whether they are willing and able to lay the foundations for mutual understanding and strengthen the solidarity between the insiders and outsiders? These are reasonable questions given the unresolved problems regarding the position of non-EU nationals in most EU countries and in the light of new migration trends (primarily an increase in migration flows). These trends are partly the legacy of Europe's colonial past and partly the result of an influx of immigrant workers and asylum-seekers. In recent times, attempts have been made to stem the flow of immigration, which means that the increase in the immigrant population is attributable to illegal immigration. The new immigrants find themselves in a very different position from their predecessors; they are not given the same level of protection by their host countries or their new employers. If they have migrated legally from other EU countries their basic social rights are guaranteed but if they come from outside the Union to work illegally, they have no rights.

About two-thirds of migrants in the European Union are non-EU nationals, with the fewest social rights. Neither they nor their children can acquire full citizenship even though many of their children are born in their new country of residence. However, these new migrants do not have a monopoly on the social problems associated with migration. Another burning issue is the degree of integration of migrants from outside the EU who are legally resident. The problem arises because, under the policies pursued by the Member States, residence is more easily acquired than citizenship. The fundamental question is this: will the European Union and its Member States guarantee citizenship rights for all people living and working in the Union, and what principles will be used to determine how these rights are granted? For the time being, it seems that citizenship has been somewhat sidelined and that the significant status is residence, as the central requirement for equality before the law, and access to social services and welfare systems.

The new influx of immigrants and the increasing number of residents of foreign origin have prompted political leaders to take measures to control the situation inside their countries and manage the inflows, using joint supranational and national policies (e.g. the Schengen agreement).

3.2.3. Work in market and non-market spheres

New forms of work

Is paid work still the most innovative and efficient form of production? Are the new forms of business creation, self-employment and 'social economy' replacing traditional forms of work? There are three reasons for the proliferation of new forms of work:

- first, the economic recession in the 1990s;
- second, the restructuring and cutbacks in the public sector;
- lastly, the deregulation of working time and work contracts, coupled with stricter rules for claiming unemployment benefit.

Sharing of household and community work

The division of labour between market and non-market, or paid and unpaid work is a product of the process of industrialization. In recent years there has been a shift from the traditional discussion of childcare services towards the role and value of home work in the broadest sense of the term. The increase in the number of women in paid work and the expansion in 'self-service society' (Gershuny 1987) have laid the foundations for a public debate on the future of the service society and the infrastructure families need if both parents work outside the home.

The growth in services for people at home, often confused with the broader category of proximity services of which they are a part, has given rise to a wealth of government initiatives in all the European countries in the 1990s. Governments supported this line primarily for employment reasons though there are other reasons, such as the new demand for services for the elderly and ill people. It is hoped that subsidies for private firms offering services to households can help bring about a more equal distribution of workload and income, and stop the spread of undeclared work.

A clear distinction emerges between two categories of home workers: one close to the self-employment model includes people such as the cleaning woman with multiple employers; and another hybrid category including people such as home-help workers, employed partly by a home-help organization and partly, when they can afford it, by the households where she actually does her work. The two types reflect two quite separate sectors of activity: 'domestic services', including everyone employed by private individuals and covered by national collective agreements for home employees; and the home-help sector, largely made up of household assistants (now home helps), family workers and para-medical staff. Increasingly, efforts are being made to expand private services, especially services provided at home.

3.2.4. Work within the life cycle

New interrelation of life and career

Wage labour is not only the dominant form of work and chief source of income; it has also become a central element in the structure of the individual's life cycle. Educational institutions and social policy schemes are closely linked with modern wage labour. This life cycle has three phases: education is the preparation for working life, after education comes paid work and after this 'active period', supposedly, retirement. In recent decades, and especially in the 1990s, this standard form of modern life cycle has undergone several changes: the length of time spent in education has increased; work, on the other hand, takes up less time; because old people retire earlier, the nature of the retirement phase of life has changed and retirement is now a third active phase. In the light of these structural changes, several researchers have come to the conclusion that the linear model of the life cycle has been replaced by a model in which different phases of the life cycle mix with each other. Suikkanen and Viinamäki (1999, 25) call this model 'the overlapping life course model'.

Ageing and working life

The increase in the average age of the population and the work-force, and the rise in the standard of living, have both had an effect on working life. The proportion of the old people in the total population will increase. They are in better condition, physically and mentally, than ever before, yet they are discriminated against in the labour market, in education and other areas of social life. Four characteristics have to be taken into account:

1) 'The elderly' are not a homogenous group.
2) During their lifetime they are constantly developing some abilities and losing others; all depends on what you are looking at. There is nothing inevitable about declining abilities.
3) Biological and physiological arguments have often been used to support the belief that our ability to work declines with age.
4) Middle-aged and old people can continue to learn and develop throughout their lives. This has been demonstrated even in relation to computer skills. For an example of the significance of the ageing population, we need look no further than the growing political awareness of older people, who are forming pressure groups to defend themselves against discrimination.

The way work is organized and distributed greatly influences older people's chances of remaining in the labour market up to retirement. From an organizational point of view it is extremely important that individuals retain a degree of control over their own work.

Lifelong learning and social programmes

It has generally been harder for the older employees to maintain their professional skills because they have not tended to take part in staff training as much as others. This often leads into a spiral that reinforces the processes of exclusion within the organization. Age, along with gender, seems to be one of the most significant and constant factors in determining which direction an employee's career will take.

3.2.5. Social infrastructure for tomorrow's workers

Working life is changing. The changes are taking place within a social infrastructure that, broadly speaking, arose in the period following the Second World War, under different social and economic conditions. They have placed an increasing strain on the welfare state as it struggles to cope with the effects of growing unemployment, an ageing population and increasing numbers of women in paid employment. Making sure that the welfare state can deliver in all these areas is becoming increasingly difficult in a number of advanced industrial societies. This is due to a number of trends.

The new service society, childcare and careers

The provision of more extensive childcare has become an increasingly topical issue in a number of countries, not only because it affects the number of women in the workforce but also because of the potential it offers for creating new forms of employment. Childcare provision in Europe varies considerably between Member States: in some countries – France and the Nordic countries, for instance – it is largely provided as a public service, whereas in other countries, such as the UK and Germany, the state does not play such a major role. Families may have to make private arrangements.

Social issues have not been studied much from the point of view of children. In view of Europe's high unemployment rate, an especially important theme is how children are affected when their parents are unemployed.

Helping people to deal with constant change

In a modern, global society, it is difficult to say with any degree of certainty which jobs are safe, or to predict how the labour market and working life will develop. From the point of view of control, the new ways of organising work make heavy demands on individuals. Even at the lowest organizational level, they have to take on a certain amount of responsibility. Knowledge and skills are considered key factors for individuals' job prospects and for the future of society. An ability to handle information effectively is the key to dealing with changing situations.

Redistributing work – An option for European societies

Sociological and psychological studies clearly indicate that the recession and structural changes of the 1990s not only affected the socialization of long-term unemployed people but also influenced the values, aspirations and behaviour of employed people in ways likely to produce some crucial changes in society. One solution to Europe's unemployment problems may be to redistribute work, to obtain a better balance between productive and reproductive work, a fairer division of work between the employed and the unemployed and, thirdly, a more balanced distribution of work, rest and leisure throughout an individual's life. Still, the idea of redistributing work has not made as much headway as expected and has given rise to a number of doubts and political struggles.

3.2.6. The need for further research

As we have seen above, European societies are having to deal with changes in their employment systems. As a rule, the term 'employment system' is used in this study to refer to both productive and reproductive work, different models of paid work and working time arrangements. It is shaped by family systems, industrial structures, welfare systems and services, social structures and the cultural values of the societies in question.

The current restructuring of European employment systems is characterized by the following trends:

- jobless growth in Western Europe;
- the spread of innovations in information and telecommunication technology;
- the increasing amount and changing nature of migration;
- segmentation of labour markets and the working environment in Europe;
- the ageing of the work force and the population at large;
- new patterns of lifelong participation in the labour market;
- an increase in self-employment and work organized along co-operative lines, including employment in third sector and private services;
- greater flexibility in working-time arrangements;
- regional and contractual variations in employment contracts and regulations;
- globalization of production, labour markets and work environments.

Thus, some issues requiring further research are:

- globalization of the economy and labour markets, and the social consequences of it;
- social differentiation and stratification in post-industrial societies;

- the need for new infrastructure needed in modern societies undergoing constant change;
- the redistribution of work, its advantages and disadvantages.

Research into globalization can be sub-divided into at least three areas:

First, the fundamental questions concerning globalization itself: How does globalization affect Europe's economy and employment systems? What kind of cultural, economic and political factors are at play in the process of globalization? Is there a specifically European answer to the challenge of globalization?

Second, the European Commission has often stressed the importance of European competitiveness in relation to the USA and Japan. Many big European companies already seem to be globally competitive, but the difficult question remains as to how globally competitive firms and industries relate to other firms and their work force. Here, the challenge is to develop socio-economic strategies that do not lead to new divisions and inequalities between export industries and home markets.

So, the research issues, in general terms are these: What kind of mutually supportive relationships exist between export industries and home markets? What can be done to strengthen these relationships? These questions are, of course, closely linked to research on differentiation and stratification, mentioned above.

Finally, globalization has brought changes in the way national economies and labour markets are regulated. It has also affected the European Union's policy line. At the same time a new, though still weak, global system of regulation appears to be emerging (WTO, ILO, MAI negotiations and so on). This raises the following questions: What kind of relationships exist between these different levels of regulation? Should certain levels of regulation be given more weight than others?

3.2.7. Bibliography

Anttila,T. (1997),Työajan lyhentäminen ja uudelleenorganisointi. 6+6 − tuntia työaikamallin toteutus suomalaisyrityksissä; in: *Työpoliittinen tutkimus* Nro 171.Työministeriö, Helsinki.

Arbejdsministerium (1996), Et godt arbejdsliv. Arbejdsministerium, København. Retrieved from http://www.am.dk/dep/galiv_0.htm on 12 May 1997.

Arbetstid,Web site: www.naring.regeringen.se/

Aronsson, G. (1994), *Samhällsomvandling och arbetsliv. Omvärldsanalys inför 2000–talet*. Arbetsmiljöinstitutet, Solna.

Aronsson, G., Kilbom, A. (eds.) (1996), *Arbete efter 45: historiska, psykologiska och fysiologiska perspektiv på äldre i arbetslivet*.Arbetslivsinstitutet, Solna.

Bang. (1997), *Thema Arbete/Pengar*, No 1/1997. Stockholms universitet.

Bastian, J. (1994),Work sharing:The reappearance of a timely idea; in: *The Political Quarterly*, 302–312. London.

Beck, U. (1997), *The Reinvention of Politics. Rethinking Modernity in the Global Social Order*. Polity Press.

Bercusson, B., Deakin, S., Koistinen, P., Kravaritou, Y., Mueckenberger, U., Supiot, A., Veneziani, B. (1996), *Manifesto for Social Europe*. ETUI. Brussels.

Bevelander, P., Carlson, B., Rojas, M. (1997), *I Krusbärslandets storstäder − Om invandrare i Stockholm, Göteborg och Malmö*.SNS-Förlag.

Bevelander, P., Carlson, B., Rojas, M. (1997),'Så skapas en etnisk underklass'; in: *Dagens Nyheter*, 20.4.1997. A 4.

Bonke, J. (1996), *Nordisk arbejdsmarkedsforskning 1993–95*, Nord 1996: 40. Nordisk Ministerråd, København.

Boreus, K. (1994), *Högervågen. Nyliberalism och kampen on språket i svensk offentlig debatt 1969–1989*.Tidens Förlag.

Bottrup, P., Hvid, H. (1995), *Et bedre arbejdsliv og øget vækst. Rapport til Arbejdsministeriet*.Arbejdsministeriet, København.

Bruun, N. (1995), *Hur förnya arbetsrätten?* Arbetsmarknad & Arbetsliv 1:2, pp.83–98.

Campbell, I. (1996), The End of Standard Working-Time? Working-time arrangements and trade unionism in a time of transition. National Key Centre in Industrial relations. Monash university. Working papers No 39.

Castells, M. (1996), *The Rise of Network Society*. Blackwell, Oxford.

Davies, A., Naschold, F., Pritchard, W., Reve, T. (1993), Evaluation report. Commissioned by the Board of the SBA Programme.

Delsen, L., Reday Mulvey, G. (eds.) (1996), *Gradual retirement in the OECD-countries: Macro and micro issues and policies*. Dartmouth Publishing company, Aldershot.

Ekstrand, L. (1996), *Arbetets död och medborgalön*. Bokförlaget Korpen. Göteborg.

Esping-Andersen, G., Korpi, W. (1986), From Poor Relief to Institutional Welfare States; in: *The Scandinavian Model: Welfare States and Welfare Research*, edited by Erikson, R. et al. Sharpe, Armonk N.Y.

ETUI (1996), *Collective Bargaining in Western Europe (1995–1996)*. Brussels.

European Commission (1993), *Growth, Competitiveness, Employment – The Challenges and Ways Forward into the 21st Century*.

European Commission (1996), *Employment in Europe 1996*, Directorate-General for Employment and Social Affairs.

European Commission (1996), Local development and employment initiatives – Lessons for territorial and local employment pacts. Working paper. November 1996–sec(96)2061.

Fajertag, G. (1996), Working Time Policies in Europe – Recent Trends. Contribution to the International Conference 'New Strategies for Everyday Life, Work, Free Time and Consumption'. Tilburg University, 12–14. December 1996.

Giddens, A. (1991), *The Consequences of Modernity*. Polity Press.

Gorz, A. (1989), *Kritik der Ökonomischen Vernunft*. Rotbuch Verlag.

Helier, A. (1992), Europe – An epilogue. In: Nelson, B., Roberts, D., Veit, W. (eds) *The Idea of Europa. Problems of National and Transnational Identity.* Berg. 1992.

Hermansson, M., Koistinen, P., Lehtonen, S., Suoranta, K. (1996), *Yksi työ – Kaksi tekijää.* Tutkimus osa-aikalisäjärjestelmän taloudellisista, sosiaalisista ja työllisyysvaikutuksista. Suomen kunnat.

Hildebrandt, V. (1997), Der Dritte Sektor – Wege aus der Arbeitsgesellschaft. In: *Krisis – Beiträge zur Kritik der Warengesellschaft.* No 19, 106–163.

Hoegelund, J. (1996), The Danish Schemes with Educational and Parental Leave. A paper presented in the seminar on Job Alternation. 28–29 November 1996. Helsinki.

Hoffman, R. (1996), On the road to lifetime working hours – some ideas to spark off discussion. Contribution to the International Conference 'New Strategies for Everyday Life, Work, Free Time and Consumption'. Tilburg University, 12–14. December 1996.

Hoffmann, R., Lapeyre, J. (eds). (1996), A Time for Working, A Time for Living. A documentation of the joint conference – the European Trade Union confederation (ETUC) and the European Trade Union Institute (ETUI). December 1994. ETUI and LRD.

Hugemark, A. (1994), *Den fängslande marknaden – Ekonomiska experter om värlfaärdsstaten.* Lund studies on social welfare. Arkiv Förlag.

Hydén, H. (1996), *Vad kommer efter lönearbetsrätten?* Arbetsmarknad & Arbetsliv 2:3, pp.157–175.

Hyman, R., Brough, I. (1975), *Social Values and Industrial Relations. A Study of Fairness and Equality.* Basil Blackwell, Oxford.

ILO (1997), Protecting the most vulnerable of today's workers. Discussion paper for Tripartitive Meeting of Experts on Future ILO Activities in the Field of Migration. ILO. Geneva.

Israel, J., Hermansson, H-E. (1996), *Det nya klasssamhället.* Ordfront. Stockholm.

Johansson, A. (1997), I vilket cirkel får du vara med? Review in: *Dagens Nyheter,* 20.4.1997.

Jolkkonen, A. (1997), Naisen paikka – Tutkimus irtisanomisuhan alaisten naisten työmarkkinastrategioista ja paikallisista työmarkkinoista. Dissertation. University of Joensuu.

Koistinen, P. (1997), *Työttömyysturvan uudistamisen tarve ja lähtökohdat.* Työpoliittinen aikakauskirja, 1/1997. pp.51–67.

Koistinen, P. (eds.) (1997), Redistributing work – An option for the European Employment System and Welfare Research programme promoting the practices of work-sharing in the European Union.

Labruyere, C. (1997), Services for persons at home: Issues of professionalization. Training & Employment. French Newsletter from CEREQ and its associated centres, No 27/spring 1997.

Lind, J. (1994), The Labour Market Reform in Denmark: Background and Perspectives – A Comment to the Role and Development of Unemployment Policy when Economic Growth is Absent and Unemployment is Present. In: Kauppinen, Timo & Köykkö, Virpi (eds.), *Transformation of the Nordic Industrial Relations in the European Context,* pp.175–199. IIRA 4th European Regional Congress Helsinki, Finland 24–26 August. Plenary 1. The Finnish Labour Relations Association, Helsinki.

Linnakangas, R. (1997), Palkkatyö modernin yhteiskunnan konstruktiona. Tutkimus työpaikan menettäneiden palkkatyöläisasemista ja työurista. Dissertation, University of Lapland.

LO-Tidningen (27 March 1997), Facta om industriavtalet. Tre nya institutioner ska bildas för att få lönebildningen inom industrin att fungera bättre. Retrieved from http://www.lo.se: 80/cgi-bin/ionews-read?showmessage=15 on 27 March 1997.

LO-Tidningen (27 March 1997), Fakta om industriavtalet. Tre nya institutioner ska bildas för att få lönebildningen inom industrin att fungera bättre. Retrieved from LO-Tidningens homepage (section 'Hetaste nyheterna'), http://www.lo.se/lotid/lotid.htm on 27 March 1997.

Mackley, J. (1996), The European Community's Interest in Working Time. A paper presented in the seminar on Job Alternation. 28–29 November 1996. Helsinki.

Matthies, H., Muckenberger, U., Offe, C., Peter, E., Raasch, S. (1994), Arbeit 2000. Anforderungen an eine Neugestaltung der Arbeitswelt – Eine Studie der Hans-Böckler-Stiftung. RoRo.

Ministry of Labour (1997), Labour Market Policy in Transition. Ministry of Labour, Copenhagen. Retrieved from http://www.am.dk./dep/lmpit.htm on 13 March 1997.

Morris, L. (1994), *Dangerous Classes – The Underclass and Social Citizenship*. Routlege 1994.

Morris, L. (1997), Globalization, migration and the nation-state: The path to a post-national Europe? In: *British Journal of Sociology*, Vol. 48, Issue No 2, 192–207.

Näsman, E., Gerber, C. von (1996), *Mamma och pappa utan jobb*. Rädda Barnen, Falun.

Nieminen, A. (1995), Towards a European Industrial Relations System? The Point of View of Equality. In: Mayes, David G. (ed.) (1995), *The Evolution of Rules for a Single European Market*. Part III Social and International Issues. Proceedings from the COST A7 Workshop in Exeter, UK. 8–11 September 1994. Office for Official Publications of the European Communities, Luxembourg (can be obtained also from www.helsinki.fi/~arniemin/euro_ir.htm).

Olsson, B. (1996), The Labour Market Measures in the Context of Economic Redundancy. A paper presented in the seminar on Job Alternation. 28–29 November 1996. Helsinki.

Olsson, B., Skanse, M. (1996), Six Hours a Day with Full Pay. The Stockholm project. Paper to be presented at the 8th International Conference on Socio-Economics. July 12–14, Geneva.

O'Neill, S. (1996), Redistributing Work: Methods and Possibilities. Australian Parliamentary Research service. (www.par18. aph.gov.au/prs/pubs/rp/rp26.htm).

Pilcher, J. (1996), Transition to and from the labour markets – Younger and older people and employment. In: *Work, Employment & Society.* Vol. 10, No 1, pp. 161–173.

Promberger, M., Rosducher, J., Seifert, R., Trinczek, R. (1995), *Beschäftigungssicherung durch Arbeitszeitverkürzung* – Tage-Woche bei Vw und Freischichten in Bergbau. Sigma Edition.

Rifkin, J. (1996), *The End of Work.* Tarher Punam. N.Y.

Rocard, M. (1995), Working document of the Committee on Social Affairs and Employment on a reduction in working hours. European Parliament. Doc EN\Dt\262\262863. 7.2.1995.

Roche, W. K., Fynes, B., Morrissey, T. (1996), Working Time and Employment: A Review of International Evidence. In: *International Labour Review,* 135:2, pp. 129–157.

Sanne, C. (1995), *Arbetets tid. Om arbetstidsreformer och konsumption i välfärdsstaten.* Carlssons. Stokholm.

Social Europe (1993), Towards a Europe of solidarity: Combating social exclusion. (by Diana Robbins) Commission of the European Communities. Supplement 4/93.

Spitzley, H. (1993), Zukunft: der Erwerbsarbeit – Zukunft: der Arbeitswissenschaft; in: *Gesellschaft für Arbeitswissenschaft u. a. (Hg.)* Arbeit- Leistung- Gesundheit, Nürnberg.

Suikkanen, A., Viinamäki, L. (1996), Ending of Work, Life Course and Labour Market Citizenship. International Working Party on Labour Market Segmentation 18th Conference on European Employment Systems and the Welfare State 9–14 July at the University of Tampere, Finland.

Suoranta, K. (1996), Work Sharing and its impacts to household economy and income transfers. A paper presented for the International working party on labour market segmentation. 9–14 July, Tampere.

Supiot, A. (1996), Perspectives of work: Introduction. In: *International Labour Review,* Vol. 135. No 6.

Therborn, G. (1995), *European Modernity and Beyond*. Sage. London.

3.3. REGULATING WORK AND WELFARE IN THE FUTURE: TOWARDS A NEW SOCIAL CONTRACT OR A NEW GENDER CONTRACT?

Summary of the study carried out by Jacqueline O'Reilly and Claudia Spee[45]

This paper looks at the origins of the different systems of labour law and social security in Europe, and the guiding principles behind them. It discusses how these have given rise to different employment systems, and focuses on the characteristic features of and changes in European systems designed to regulate work and social welfare. Two key developments are identified: increasing decentralization of collective bargaining and the shifting balance between flexibility at work and employment security. Other trends are noted: decentralization and outsourcing in state monopolies and attempts to develop new forms of welfare and care provision.

As we approach the end of the century, social conditions have changed enormously. For some people, their career has become something of a 'patchwork', combining a variety of jobs and employment statuses in the course of their working life. However, traditional forms of employment and social security systems tend to have been based on the male breadwinner model, in which the male head of household had a job for life. To understand how common trends are affecting national systems, we need to look at them in relation to employment systems; we see that it is not possible, for example, to explain how work will be organized in future solely in terms of production.

---

[45] Both are researchers at the Nissenschaftszentrum Berlin für Sozialforschung.

3.3.1. Labour regulation

The debate on flexibility in the labour market has drawn attention to one of the major issues for employment regulation. In recent years, the focus has been on the rigidities created by mechanisms designed to protect jobs and collective bargaining arrangements. Skill flexibility and multi-skilling have also been topical issues. Debate has arisen over the adequacy of existing training systems, and firms can opt out of them too easily.

Regulation can occur at four basic levels:

- at *national level* through legislation that applies to everyone;
- at the *branch or industry level* through collective agreements that apply to all firms in a particular category or a whole industry;
- at the *plant or company level* through local collective agreements; and
- at the purely *individual level* through employment contracts between employers and employees.

Collective bargaining systems differ from country to country, depending on whether they have a strong, moderate or weak tradition. We can distinguish between three main types of regulatory system. First, *statist flexibility* is the type found in countries with a strong statutory and weak collective bargaining system such as France and to some degree Spain. In such countries, employment conditions tend to be governed by law and the unions play only a minor role. *Negotiated flexibility* is found in systems with moderate statutory regulation and strong or moderate collective bargaining traditions such as Sweden and Germany, as well as the Netherlands and Ireland. The key to the system's success is the level at which negotiations take place. In Sweden, for instance, the subsidiarity principle is applied. *Individualized flexibility* is found in countries with a minimal level of statutory regulation and weak collective bargaining, such as the UK, where, it could be argued, flexibility is increasingly individualized. Despite the differences between regulatory systems in Europe, there is a general shift towards decentralized bargaining and more flexible implementation.

One of the key issues for the regulation of work in the future is the *relationship between standard and non-standard employment*, or between core and marginalized workers, and those excluded from work. Deregulation *'generates new, albeit different kinds, of rules'*. The notion of 'flexicurity' has been introduced in an attempt to stem the rising tide of job insecurity. In France, the adoption of the Robien law has generated considerable controversy, drawing both criticism and praise. The law sets out to encourage firms to use working time reductions to employ more staff by reducing social costs over a period of seven years.

There is little prospect of a social democratic or neo-corporatist Europe redistributing resources to the 'losers' as markets become freer. More likely is a neo-pluralist social Europe in which temporary coalitions of interests prompt governments to join together in support of individual social measures at European level, while other social issues are left to national or regional authorities, or are dealt with through collective bargaining.

3.3.2. Social welfare regulation

Some researchers divide welfare states into three categories: *liberal, conservative* and *social-democratic*. On the basis of this division, 18 countries have been categories according to the degree of decommodification, social stratification and the relationship between the state and the market. Decommodification refers to the cash-wage nexus, i.e. the extent to which the state intervenes in redistribution so that *'a person can maintain a livelihood without being dependent on the market'*.

Alternative approaches have focused on the ideological basis of the welfare system. Lewis and Ostner divide social policy systems into strong, moderate and weak *'breadwinner' systems*

(Lewis 1992). These categories refer to the extent to which taxation and social-transfer systems are geared towards a society in which households are composed of a single, full-time employed, male earner with inactive dependants; strong breadwinner systems tend to treat women as dependent on male earners, rather than as individuals. Sainsbury (1996) more critically argues that the concepts of 'decommodification' or 'breadwinner' are too simplistic to capture the complexity and paradoxes found within welfare regimes. She argues that welfare states operate on several principles simultaneously, and identifies five such principles: maintenance, care, citizenship, need, and labour market performance or status. We would argue that the evidence from these debates indicates first, that welfare regimes are not converging and second, future reform and regulation of these systems is likely to produce divergent trajectories, with implications for the future of work.

3.3.3. Public-private partnerships and new forms of caring and employment

In a number of European countries the nature of the state's monopoly over welfare provision is gradually changing. European welfare systems currently face a range of problems: from the stubbornly high and rising number of people without work to the gloomy demographic forecasts for the early part of the next century when a disproportionate number of elderly people are expected to exit the labour market. The pressure to reduce public spending or, at least, use limited public resources more effectively has given rise to attempts to develop new forms of public-private partnerships. There have also been attempts to develop policy solutions that are nearer to the market, more 'customer-orientated', and therefore potentially more effective. Although some of these developments have been praised for their innovativeness and effectiveness, there are also concerns about potential weaknesses: questions have been raised regarding the quality of the services provided by these new arrangements; some suspect that regional action has been overplayed and that the structural influence of supra-national or national institutions is often underestimated.

In conclusion, we see that despite universal pressures for societies to modernize and adapt, in many cases nationally specific solutions are being developed. In order to understand how the future will unfold we need to adopt an employment system perspective. Such an approach provides a prism through which we can examine the changing relationship between the fields of economic production, social reproduction and regulation. This approach can also be used for future research to enable us to identify the role of actors at local, national and supra-national levels.

3.3.4. In search of a new social contract or a revised gender contract?

Women's entry into waged employment produces a growing 'contradiction of equality' as they are increasingly involved in competitive relations based on the principle of individual merit and citizenship, which is largely defined with reference to institutionalized male norms. In her analysis of Sweden, Hirdmann (1988) argues that economic and political pressures eroded the 'housewife contract', which was replaced by the 'equality contract' of the 1960s. This contract normalized women's employment through institutional reform and the expansion of the welfare state.

Gender is increasingly conceptualized as a process which permeates institutions and social relations *throughout* the employment system, though gender-blind analyses still predominate when women are not the self-evident focus of the research.

The challenge for the future will be to establish a new social contract in the sphere of labour and social welfare regulation. In the past, these sought to knit people into the fabric of the nation.

In the future too, we must devise forms of regulation that prevent further polarization of society, provide new forms of social cohesion and solidarity between generations, between women and men and between the working poor and the rich. These changes are likely to give rise to a new, or at least revised, form of the gender contract, specifying the relations and rights between men and women in society. But the progressive influence of this new contract will depend on the degree to which citizenship rights for equality are extended to the private as well as the public domain.

3.3.5. Bibliography

Abraham, K.G., Houseman, S.N. (1994), Does Employment Protection Inhibit Labor Market Flexibility? In: Blank, R. (ed.), pp.59–93.

Adam, G., Reynaud, J.-D., Verdier, J.-M. (1972), *La Négociation Collective en France*; Paris: Les Editions Ouvriers.

Addison, J.T., Siebert, W.S. (1994), Recent developments in Social Policy in the New European Union; in: *Industrial and Labour Relations Review*, Vol. 48, No 1, pp.5–27.

Anxo, D., Storrie, D. (1997), *Regulating Working Time Transitions in Sweden*, mimeo.

Auer, A., Demmke, Ch., Polet, R. (1996), *Civil Services in the Europe of Fifteen: Current Situation and Prospects*; Maastricht: European Institute of Public Administration.

Aznar, G. (1997), Réduction du temps de travail: la loi Robien; in: *Futuribles*, 217 fév, pp.15–28.

Bäcker, G. (1995), Altersarmut – Frauenarmut: Dimensionen eines sozialen Problems und sozialpolitische Reformoptionen; in: Hanesch (Hrsg.), pp.375–403.

Barbier, J.-C., Nadel, H. (1996), L'évolution des systèmes de protection sociale en Europe. Crises des Etats providence et reconfiguration; in: *Revue Française des Affaires Sociales*, janvier–mars.

Beaujolin, F. (1997), *Impacts sur les relations sociales des perspectives de gestion territorialisée des enjeux de l'emploi*, mimeo.

Béhar, P. (1997), Réduction du temps de travail et emploi: du bon usage de la loi Robien; in: *Futuribles* No 221 juin., pp.9–54.

Bercusson, B., Deakin, S., Koistinen, P., Kravaritou, Y., Mückenberger, U., Supiot, A., Veneziani, B. (1996), *A Manifesto for Social Europe*; Brussels: European Trade Union Institute.

Blank, R. (ed.) (1994), *Social Protection versus Economic Flexibility. Is there a trade-off?* Chicago and London: The University of Chicago Press.

Blyton, P., Trinczek, R. (1997), Renewed interest in working-sharing? Assessing recent developments in Germany; in: *Industrial Relations Journal*, Vol. 28, pp.3–13.

Bosch, G. (1996), *Der Arbeitsmarkt bis zum Jahre 2010. Ökonomische und Soziale Entwicklung*; Graue Reihe des Instituts Arbeit und Technik 96/4.

Boulin, J-Y., Cette, G., Dauchot, M. et al. (1996), La réduction du temps de travail en France; in: *Futuribles*, No 205, pp.21–37.

Brocas, A.-M., Hadolph, P. (1995), Monopole ou concurrence en matière de protection sociale; in: *Droit Social*, septembre–octobre.

Bruun, N. (1994), The Transformation of the Nordic Industrial Relations; in: Kauppinen, T. and Köykkö, V. (eds.), pp.15–43.

Bruun, N. (1995), Hur förnya arbetsrätten? In: *Arbetsmarknad & Arbetsliv*, Vol.1, No 2, pp.83–89.

Büchtemann, C.F., Neumann, H. (Hg.) (1990), *Mehr Arbeit durch weniger Recht? Chancen und Risiken der Arbeitsmarktflexibilisierung*; Berlin: Edition Sigma.

Bullmann, U. (1996), Aufbruch aus dem Zentralstaat? Der europäische Einfluss auf die subnationale Politik in Grossbritannien; in: *Österriche Zeitschrift für Politikwissenschaft*, Jg. 25, H. 3, pp.261–278.

Bullmann, U., Heinze, R.G. (Hrsg.) (1997), *Regionale Modern-isierungspolitik. Nationale und internationale Perspektiven*; Opladen: Leske + Buderich.

Bundesministerium für Arbeit und Soziales (1992), *Die Effizienz der Arbeitsmarktverwaltung. Organizationsanalyse*, Wien, Forschungsberichte aus Sozial- und Arbeitsmarktpolitik No 45.

Bundesministerium für Arbeit und Sozialordnung (1996), *Euro Atlas*. Soziale Sicherheit im Vergleich; Bonn: Bundes-ministerium für Arbeit und Sozialordnung; (Provides an over-view of legal regulation of social security provisions in 15 member states), also available under http://www.de/eu_atlas/index.html.

Cases, C., Saunier, J.-M., Volovitch, P. (1996), Le financement de la protection sociale en Europe; in: *Solidarité santé* – Etudes statistiques, janvier–mars.

Cebrián et al. (1997), *Working time in Spain*; mimeo.

Cette, G. (1997), La loi Robien et la réduction du temps de travail; in: *Futuribles* No 217 fév, pp.29–32.

Coyle, G. (1997), The nature and value of future studies or do futures have a future? In: *Futures*, Vol. 29, No 1, pp.77–94.

Crouch, C. (1993), *Industrial Relations and European State Transitions*; Oxford: Clarendon Press.

Crouch, C., Traxler, F. (eds.) (1995), *Organized Industrial Relations in Europe: What Future?* Aldershot: Avebury.

Daly, M. (1997), The Case of Welfare State Change and Transition: Some Feminist Approaches Reviewed; paper presented to the 33rd World Congress of Sociology, July 7–11, University of Cologne.

Daly, M. (1997a), Post What? Theorising welfare state change; in: *Acta Sociologica*, Vol. 40, No 2.

Daly, M. (1997b), Welfare states under pressure: Cash benefits in European welfare states over the last ten years; in: *Journal of European Social Policy*, Vol. 7, No 2, pp.129–146.

Daune-Richard, A-K (1998), How does the 'societal effect' shape the use of part-time work in France, the UK and Sweden? In: O'Reilly, J., Fagan, C., *Part-time Prospects*, London: Routledge.

Davidson, A. (1997), Regional Politics: The European Union and Citizenship; in: *Citizenship Studies*, Vol. 1, No 1, pp.33–55.

de Foucauld, J.B. (1995), *Le financement de la protection sociale*, La Documentation Française.

de Vroom, B., Naschold, F. (1994), The Dialectics of Work and Welfare; in: Naschold and de Vroom (eds.), pp.1–17.

Dercksen, W.J., de Koning, J. (1996), The New Public Employment System in the Netherlands (1991–1994); WZB discussion paper FS I 96–201.

Düe, D. (1996), Weniger arbeiten, zukunftsfähig leben. Schlussfolgerungen aus dem VW-Modell; in: *Blätter für Deutsche und Internationale Politik*, pp.437–447.

Due, J., Madsen, S.J., Jensen, S.C., Petersen, L.K. (1994), *The Survival of the Danish Model. A Historical Sociological Analysis of the Danish System of Collective Bargaining*; Copenhagen: Jurist-ogOkonomforbundets Forlag, DJOF Publishing.

Dumont, J.-P. (1995), Les systèmes de protection sociale en Europe; in: *Economica*, Paris.

Elander, I. (1996), Central-government relations and regionalism in Sweden; in: *Oesterriche Zeitschrift für Politikwissenschaft*, Jg. 25, H. 3, pp.279–294.

Esping-Andersen, G. (1990), *The Three Worlds of Welfare Capitalism*; Cambridge: Polity Press.

Esping-Andersen, G. (ed.) (1996), *Welfare States in Transition. National Adaptions in Global Economies*; London: Sage.

European Commission (1996), *Employment in Europe*; Luxembourg: EG.

Euzéby, A. (1996), Les impôts et le financement de la Protection Sociale; in: *Les cahiers français*, No 274, second quarter. 1996.

Faber, G., Schippers, J. (1997), *Flexibilisering van de arbeid*; Bussum: Couthinho.

Fagan, C., Plantenga, J., Rubery, J. (1995), Does Part-Time Work Promote Sex Equality? A Comparative Analysis of the Netherlands and the UK; Berlin: WZB discussion paper FS I 95–203.

Farnham, D., Horton, S., Barlow, J., Hondeghem, A. (ed.) (1996), *New Public Managers in Europe. Public Servants in Transition*; Houndmills: Macmillan Press.

Ferner, A., Hyman, R. (eds.) (1992), *Industrial Relations in the New Europe*; Oxford: Blackwell Publishers.

Finger, D. (1997), Service cheques in Europe – A model for Germany? Employment effects and macro-economic costs: five scenarios, WZB discussion paper FS I 97–201a.

Franzmeyer, F., Lindlar, L., Trabold, H. (1996), *Employment and social policies under international constrains*; Berlin: Deutsches Institut für Wirtschaftsforschung.

Gallie, D. (1978), *In search of the new working class. Automation and social integration within the capitalist enterprise*; Cambridge: Cambridge University Press.

Geuer, W. (1997), Die Wurzeln der Teamorganization und ihre Bedeutung für das 'AA 2000'; in: *Arbeit und Beruf*, 5/1997, pp.129–131.

Goetschy, J. (1994), A further comment on Wolfgang Streeck's European Social Policy after Maastricht; in: *Economic and Industrial Democracy*, Vol. 15, No 3, pp.477–485.

Gold, M., Hall, M. (1994), Statutory European Works Councils: The Final Countdown? In: *Industrial Relations Journal*, Vol. 25, No 3, pp.177–186.

Gräbe, S. (Hg.) (1995), *Private Haushalte und neue Arbeitsmodelle*; Frankfurt/Main, New York: Campus Verlag.

Gregg, P., Wadsworth, J. (1995), Gender, Households and Access to Employment; in: Humphries, J., Rubery, J. (ed.), pp.345–364.

Hall, P., Franzese, R. (1997), Mixed Signals: Central Bank Independence, Co-ordinated Wage Bargaining and European Monetary Union unpublished manuscript, paper presented at the WZB, Berlin April.

Hanesch, Walter (Hrsg.) (1995), *Sozialpolitische Strategien gegen Armut*; Opladen: Westdeutscher Verlag.

Hartz, P. (1994), *Jeder Arbeitsplatz hat ein Gesicht. Die Volkswagen-Lösung*; Frankfurt/New York: Campus Verlag.

Heinzemann, B. (1996), Frankreich. Förderung von Teilzeit durch Dienstleistungsschecks; in: *KND-Kurzer Nachrichtendienst*, 96/10, p.4.

Hoff, A. (1994), *Kurzsabbatical. Möglichkeiten zur Arbeitsumverteilung auf der betrieblichen Ebene. Gutachten im Auftrag der Berliner Senatsverwaltung für Arbeit und Frauen*, Berlin, Schriftenreihe der Senatsverwaltung für Arbeit und Frauen, Band 3.

Hoffmann, S. (1997), Frankreich. Arbeitszeitgesetz unerwartet erfolgreich; in: *Bundesarbeitsblatt*, 5/1997, p.20.

Hollingsworth, J.R., Schmitter, P.C., Streeck W. (eds.) (1994), *Governing capitalist economies. Performance and control of economic sectors*; New York: Oxford University Press.

Humphries, J., Rubery, J. (1984), The reconstitution of the supply side of the labour market; the relative autonomy of social reproduction; in: *Cambridge Journal of Economics*, 1984, No 8, pp.331–346.

Humphries, J., Rubery, J. (ed.) (1995), *The Economics of Equal Opportunities*; Manchester: EOC.

Jensen, S.C., Jesper, D., Madsen, S.J. (1994), The Scandinavian Model in Europe – The Choice of IR-roles for the Labour Market Parties at National and EU Levels; in: Kauppinen, T. and Köykkö, V. (eds.), pp.45–67.

Jerger, J., Spermann, A. (1996), Lösungsansätze zur Beseitigung von Fehlanreizen für Langzeitarbeitslose, in: Steiner and Zimmermann (Hrsg.), pp.109–134.

Kauppinen, T. (1994), *The Transformation of Labour Relations in Finland*; Helsinki: Ministry of Labour, Labour Policy Studies No 81.

Kauppinen, T. (1997), *Labour Relations in Finland*; Helsinki: Ministry of Labour.

97

Kauppinen, T., Köykkö (eds.) (1994), Transformation of the Nordic Industrial Relations in the European Context. IIRA 4th European Regional Congress Helsinki, Finland 24–26 August, Plenary 1; Helsinki: The Finnish Labour Relations Association.

Keller, B. (1996), Arbeit und sozialstaatliche Ordnung in Europa; in: *Gewerkschaftliche Monatshefte*, 11–12/96, pp.724–731.

Kitschelt, H., Lange, P., Marks, G., Stephens, J.D. (eds.) (1997), *Continuity and Change in Contemporary Capitalism*; Cambridge: Cambridge University Press.

Kjellberg, A. (1992), Sweden: Can the Model Survive? In: Ferner, A., Hyman, R. (eds).

Knigge, J.A., Rijnbout, M.J. (1995), *Service Vouchers. An analysis of the job creation potential and feasibility of service vouchers in the Netherlands*, Zoetermeer: EIM/ Labour Research.

Knuth, M. (1996), *Drehscheiben im Strukturwandel. Agenturen für Mobilitäts-, Arbeits- und Strukturförderung*; Berlin: edition Sigma.

Knutsen, P. (1997), Corporatist Tendencies in the Euro-Polity: The EU Directive of 22 September 1994, on European Works Councils; in: *Economic and Industrial Democracy*, Vol. 18, pp.289–323.

Köykkö, V. (1994), *Työnantajien muutuvat strategiat*. Suomalaista ja pohjoismaista työnantajapolitiikkaa 1980 – ja 1990-luvulla. Työpoliittinen tutkimus No 75. Työministeriö, Helsinki.

Kvist, J., Torfing, J. (1996), Changing Welfare State Models; Copenhagen: Centre for Welfare State Research, Working Paper 5.

Lange, P. (1992), The Politics of the Social Dimension; in: Sbragia, A. M.(ed.), pp.225–256.

Leibfried, S., Voges, W. (Hrsg.) (1992), Armut im modernen Wohlfahrtsstaat; *Kölner Zeitschrift für Soziologie und Sozialpsychologie*, Sonderheft 32/1992, Opladen: Westdeutscher Verlag.

Lewis, J. (1992), Gender and the development of welfare regimes; in: *Journal of European Social Policy*, Vol. 2, No 3, pp.159–173.

Lewis, J., Ostner, I. (1994), *Gender and the Evolution of European Social Policies*; Bremen: ZeS-Arbeitspapier No 4/94.

L'Horty, Y., Méary, R., Sobczack, N. (1994), Le coin salarial en France depuis 1970; in: *Économie et Prévision*, No 115.

Locke, R.M., Kochan, T.A., Piore, M.J. (1995), *Employment relations in a changing world economy*; Cambridge: MIT Press.

Mahnkopf, B. (1996), Gewerkschaften als Moderatoren im Standortwettbewerb? In: *Österreichische Zeitschrift für Sozialforschung*, Sonderband 3:Vernetzung undVereinnahmung, S.57–80, Opladen: Westdeutscher Verlag.

Maillard, D. (1995), Financement de la protection sociale: quel est le problème? In: *Chroniques Economiques – SEDEIS*, No 9, September.

Marginson, P. (1992), European Integration and Transnational Management-Union Relations in the Enterprise; in: *British Journal of Industrial Relations*, Vol. 30, No 4, pp.530–545.

Masson, A. (1995), Assurance sociale et assurance privée; in: *Risques*, No 24, octobre–décembre.

Matthies, H., Mückenberger, U., Offe, C., Peter, E., Raasch, S. (1994), *Arbeit 2000: Anforderungen an eine Neugestaltung der Arbeitswelt*; Hamburg: Rowohlt.

Matzner, E. (1997), Die Krise des Wohlfahrtsstaates. Eine Neubetrachtung (frei) nach Schumpeter und Morgenstern; in: *Der Öffentliche Sektor – Forschungsmemoranden, 23.* Jg., Heft 1/97, pp.1–31.

McLaughlin, E. (1994), Flexibility or Polarization? In: White, M. (ed.). *Unemployment and Public Policy in a Changing Labour Market.* London: PSI.

McLaughlin, E. (1995), Gender and Egalitarianism in the British Welfare State; in: Humphries, J., Rubery, J. (ed.), pp.291–312.

Ministry of Social Affairs and Employment of the Netherlands (1996), *The Dutch welfare state from an international and economic perspective*; The Hague: Ministry of Social Affairs and Employment of the Netherlands.

MIRE (1995, 1996), *Comparer les systèmes de protection sociale en Europe.*

Mommsen, W.J., Mock, W. (1981), *The Emergence of the Welfare State in Britain and Germany 1850–1950*; London: Croom Helm.

Mósesdóttir, L. (1995), The state and the egalitarian, ecclesiastical and liberal regimes of gender relations; in: *British Journal of Sociology*, Vol. 46, No 4, pp.623–642.

Mosley, H., Speckesser, S. (1997), Market Share and Market Segment of Public Employment Services; WZB discussion paper.

Naschold, F., de Vroom (eds.) (1994), *Regulating Employment and Welfare. Company and National Policies of Labour Force Participation at the End of Worklife in Industrial Countries*, Berlin, New York: de Gruyter.

Nieminen, A. (1995), Towards a European Industrial Relations System? The Point of View of Equality; in: Mayes, David G. (ed.) (1995), *The Evolution of Rules for a Single European Market.* Part III Social and International Issues.

Nieminen, A. (1997), Labour Market Regulation and Industrial Relations in Three Nordic Countries. Literature Survey on the Future of Work for the European Commission (DGV), preliminary working. (www.helsinki.fi\-arniemin\).

Nordli Hansen, M. (1997), The Scandinavian Welfare State Model: The Impact of the Public Sector on Segregation and Gender Equality; in: *Work, Employment & Society*, Vol. 11, No 1, pp.83–89.

O'Connell, P., McGinnity, F. (1996), What works? Who works? The Impact of Active Labour Market Programmes on the Employment Prospects of Young People in Ireland; Berlin: WZB discussion paper FS I 96–207.

O'Connell, P., McGinnity, F. (1997), Regulating Working Time Transitions in Ireland; working paper.

O'Conner, J.S. (1973), *Fiscal Crisis of the State*; New York: St. James Press.

O'Conner, J.S. (1993), Gender, class and citizenship in the comparative analysis of welfare state regimes: Theoretical and methodological issues; in: *British Journal of Sociology*, Vol. 44, No 3, pp.501–518.

O'Conner, J.S. (1996), From women in the welfare state to gendering welfare regimes; in: *Current Sociology*, Vol. 44, No 2,. pp.1–130.

OECD (1993), *Local initiatives for employment creation. Partnerships: The key to job creation.* Experiences from OECD Countries, Paris.

OECD (1994), *Employment Outlook*, OECD Paris.

OECD (1996), *Ageing in OECD Countries. A Critical Policy Challenge*; Social Policy Studies No 20, OECD Paris.

OECD (1996a), *Ireland. Local Partnerships and Social Innovation.* Prepared by Professor Charles Sabel and the LEED Programme, OECD Paris.

OECD (1996b), *Networks of Enterprises and Local Development. Competing and Co-operating in Local Productive Systems*, OECD Paris.

OECD (1996c), *The Public Employment Service: Austria, Germany, Sweden*, OECD Paris.

Offe, C. (1984), *Contradictions of the welfare state.* Hutchinson.

Offe, C. (1985), *Disorganized capitalism, contemporary transformations of works and politics*; Oxford: Polity.

Oppen, M. (1994), Modernisierung als Privatisierung. Folgen für den Öffentlichen Sektor und die Frauen im Westen; in: *Das Argument*, 204/1994, pp.185–198.

O'Reilly, J. (1994), *Banking on flexibility. A comparison of flexible employment in retail banking in Britain and France*; Aldershot: Avebury.

O'Reilly, J. (1996), Arbeitsmarkt, Arbeitsentgelt und Arbeitszeit von Frauen in den Mitgliedstaaten der Europäischen Union; in: Piepenschneider, M. (Hrsg.); pp.63–74.

O'Reilly, J. (1996), Theoretical considerations in cross-national employment research; in: *Sociological Review Online.* 1, 1: <http://www.socresonline.org.uk/socresonline/1/1/2.html>

O'Reilly, J. (ed.) (1997), Regulating Working Time and Employment Transitions in Europe: A comparison of France, Germany, Sweden, Spain, Ireland, the Netherlands and the UK; WZB discussion paper.

O'Reilly, J., Bothfeld, S. (1996), Labour market transitions and part-time work, Focus article; in: *InfoMisep*, Commission of the European Union, Brussels.

O'Reilly, J., Bothfeld, S. (1997), *Working Time Transitions in Germany*, mimeo.

O'Reilly, J., Fagan, C. (ed.) (1998), *Part-time Prospects: International comparison of part-time work in Europe, North America and the Pacific Rim*; London: Routledge.

O'Reilly, J., Reissert, B., Eichener, V. (1996), European Regulation of Social Standards: Social Security, Working Time, Workplace Participation, Occupational Health and Safety; in: Schmid, G., O'Reilly, J., Schömann, K. (eds.), pp.868–898.

Orloff, A. (1993), Gender and the social rights of citizenship: The comparative analysis of gender relations and welfare states; in: *American Sociological Review*, Vol. 58, No 3, pp.303–328.

Orloff, A. (1996), Gender in the welfare state; in: *American Review of Sociology*, Vol. 22, pp.51–78.

Pakulski, J. (1997), Cultural Citizenship; in: *Citizenship Studies*, Vol. 1, No 1, pp.73–86.

Pallier, B., Bonoli, G. (1995), Entre Bismark et Beveridge. 'Crises' de la Sécurité Sociale et politique(s); in: *Revue française de sciences politiques*, August.

Pankoke, E., Sachsse, Ch. (1992), Zum deutschen Weg in die industrielle Moderne; in: Leibfried, S., Voges, W. (Hrsg.), pp.149–173.

Passeron, H. (1997), Réduction du temps de travail et emploi: du bon usage de la loi Robien; in: *Futuribles*, No.221 June, pp.39–54.

Pennings, F.J.L. (1996), *Flexibilisering van het sociaal recht*, (Flexibilization of Social Law); Deventer: Kluwer.

Peschel, K. (ed.) (1997), Regional growth and regional policy within the framework of European integration. Proceedings of a conference on the occasion of 25 years Institute for Regional Research at the University of Kiel 1995; Heidelberg: Physica-Verlag.

Pfau-Effinger, B. (1998), Culture or structure as explanations for differences in part-time work in Germany, Finland and the Netherlands? In: O'Reilly and Fagan op. Cit.

Piepenschneider, M. (Hrsg.) (1996), *Frauen in der Europäischen Union*; Baden-Baden: Nomos.

Pierson, P. (1994), *Dismantling the Welfare State? Reagan, Thatcher and the Politics of Retrenchment*; Cambridge: Cambridge University Press.

Pinker, R. (1992), Armut, Sozialpolitik, Soziologie. Der Englische Weg von der Industriellen Revolution zum Modernen Wohlfahrtsstaat; in: Leibfried, S. and Voges, W. (Hrsg.), pp.124–148.

Pixley, J. (1993), *Citizenship and Employment. Investigating Post-Industrial Options*, Cambridge: University Press.

Prigge, W., Ronneberger, K. (1996), Globalisierung und Regionalisierung. Zur Auflösung Frankfurts in die Region; in: *Österreichische Zeitschrift für Soziologie*, Jg. 21, H. 2, pp.129–138.

Proceedings from the COST A7 Workshop in Exeter, UK (8–11 September 1994). Office for Official Publications of the European Communities, Luxembourg (can be obtained also from http://www.helsinki.fi/~arniemin/euro_ir.htm).

Quack, S. (1993), *Dynamik der Teilzeit. Implikationen für die soziale Sicherung von Frauen*; Berlin: edition sigma.

Quack, S., Maier, F. (1994), From state socialism to market economy – Women's employment in East Germany; in: *Environment and Planning A*, Vol. 26, No 8, pp.1171–1328.

Quack, S., O'Reilly, J., Hildebrandt, S. (1995), Structuring change. Training and recruitment in Germany, Britain and France; in: *The International Journal of Human Resource Management*, Vol. 6, No 4, pp.759–794.

Rabe, B. (1995), Implementation wirtschaftsnaher Arbeitsmarkt-politik. Lohnkostenzuschüsse nach paragraph 249h AFG in Berlin und Sachsen; Berlin: WZB discussion paper FS 195–206.

Rapport, Boissonnat (1995), *Le travail dans 20 ans*, Ed. Odile Jacob – La Documentation Française, Paris.

Rehn, 0. (1996), *Corporatism and industrial competitiveness in small European states: Austria, Finland and Sweden, 1945–95*; Oxford: Oxford University Press.

Rifkin, J. (1995), *Das Ende der Arbeit und ihre Zukunft*, Frankfurt/New York: Campus Verlag.

Robins, P.K. (1985), A comparison of the labor supply findings from the four negative income tax experiments; in: *The Journal of Human Resources*, Vol. 20, pp.567–582.

Rogowski, R., Schmid, G. (1997), Reflexive Deregulierung – Ein Ansatz zur Dynamisierung des Arbeitsmarktes; WZB discussion paper.

Rosdücher, J., Seifert, H. (1994), *Die Einführung der '4-Tage-Woche' in der Volkswagen AG. Modell für eine beschäftigungssichernde Arbeitszeitpolitik? Expertize im Auftrag der Berliner Senatsverwaltung für Arbeit und Frauen*, Berlin, Schriftenreihe der Senatsverwaltung Arbeit und Frauen, No 4.

Rossi, M., Sartori, E. (1995), *Ripensare la solidarieta*, Locarno, Armando Dado.

Rubery, J. (1994), The British Production Regime; in: *Economy and Society*, Vol. 23, No 3, pp.335–354.

Rubery, J. (1998), Part-Time Work: A threat to Labour Standards? In: O'Reilly, J. and Fagan, C. (ed).

Rubery, J., Fagan, C. (1995), Gender segregation in societal context; in: *Work, Employment and Society*, Vol. 9, No 2, pp.213–240.

Ruivo, M. et al. (1998), Why is part-time work so low in Spain and Portugal? In: O'Reilly and Fagan (ed.). op. Cit.

Ryberg, L., Bruun, N. (1996), An Overview of Industrial Relations Research in the Nordic Countries: Institutions and

Trends; in: *European Journal of Industrial Relations*, Vol. 2, No 1, pp.93–112.

S.Z.W. (1997), *Bill on Flexibility and Security*; Den Haag: Ministerie van Sociale Zaken en Werkgelegenheid, S.Z.W, April.

S.Z.W. (1995), *Flexibiliteit en Zekerheid*; Nota van de Minister van Sociale Zaken en Werkgelegenheid, S.Z.W, December.

Sainsbury, D. (1993), Dual welfare and sex segregation of access to social benefits: Income maintenance policies in the UK, the US, the Netherlands and Sweden; in: *Journal of Social Policy*, Vol. 22, No 1, pp.69–98.

Sainsbury, D. (ed.) (1994), *Gendering Welfare States*; London: Sage.

Sainsbury, D. (1996), *Gender, Equality and Welfare States*; Cambridge: Cambridge University Press.

Sbragia, A.M. (ed.) (1992), *Euro-Politics. Institutions and Policy-making in the New European Community*; Washington, D.C.: The Brookings Institution.

Schäffers, B. (1992), Zum öffentlichen Stellenwert von Armut im sozialen Wandel der Bundesrepublik Deutschland; in: *Leibfried and Voges (1992)*, pp.104–123.

Scharpf, F. (1993), Von der Finanzierung der Arbeitslosigkeit zur Subventionierung niedriger Erwerbseinkommen; in: *Gewerkschaftliche Monatshefte*, Heft 7/1993, pp.433–443.

Schiller, B. (1993), The Future of the Nordic Model of Labour Relations; in: *The Future of the Nordic Model of Labour Relations – Three Reports on Internationalization and Industrial Relations*, pp.7–91. Nord 1993: 36. Nordic Council of Ministers, Copenhagen.

Schmähl, Winfried (Hg.) (1993), *Mindestsicherung im Alter: Erfahrungen, Herausforderungen, Strategien*; Frankfurt/Main, New York: Campus Verlag.

Schmähl, W. (1993a), Übergang zu Staatsbürger-Grundrenten. Ein Beitrag zu Deregulierung in der Alterssicherung? In: Schmähl (Hg.), pp.265–361.

Schmid, G., Reissert, B., Bruche, G. (1992), *Unemployment Insurance and Active Labour Market Policy: An International*

Comparison of Financing Systems; Detroit: Wayne State University Press.

Schmid, G. (1993), Übergänge in die Vollbeschäftigung. Formen und Finanzierung einer zukunftgerechten Arbeitsmarktpolitik; Berlin: WZB discussion paper FS I 93–208.

Schmid, G., O'Reilly, J., Schömann, K. (ed.) (1996), *International Handbook of Labour Market Policy and Evaluation*; Cheltenham: Edgar Elgar.

Schmid, G., O'Reilly, J., Schömann, K. (1996a), Theory and Methodology of Labour Market Policy and Evaluation: An Introduction; in: Schmid, G., O'Reilly, J. and Schömann, K. (eds.), pp.1–33.

Schmid, G., Helmer, M. (Mitarb.) (1997), The Dutch Employment Miracle. A comparison of employment systems in the Netherlands and Germany; Berlin: WZB discussion paper FS 197–202.

Schmid, J. (1996), *Wohlfahrtsstaaten im Vergleich. Soziale Sicherungssysteme in Europa: Organization, Finanzierung, Leistung und Probleme*; Opladen: Leske + Buderich.

Schröder, J., van Suntum, U., Bertelsmann, Stiftung (Hrsg.) (1996), *Internationales Beschäftigungs-Ranking 1996*; Gütersloh: Verlag Bertelsmann Stiftung.

Schunter-Kleemann, S. (Hg.) (1992), *Herrenhaus Europa – Geschlechterverhältnisse im Wohlfahrtsstaat*; Berlin: edition Sigma.

Schunter-Kleemann, S. (1992a), Wohlfahrtsstaat und Patriarchat – Ein Vergleich Europäischer Länder; in: Schunter-Kleemann, S. (Hg.) (1992), pp.141–327.

Smith, M., Rubery, J., Fagan, C. (1997), *Working Time Transitions in the UK Labour Market*; mimeo.

Soskice, D. (1997), Divergent Production Regimes. Coordinated and Uncoordinated Market Economies in the 1980s and 1990s; in: Kitschelt, H., Lange, P., Marks, G., Stephens, J.D. (eds.).

Spermann, A. (1994), Das Bürgergeld – Ein sozial- und beschäftigungspolitisches Wundermittel? In: *Sozialer Fortschritt*, 43. Jg., Heft 5, pp.105–111.

Steiner, V., Zimmermann, K.F. (Hrsg.) (1996), *Soziale Sicherung und Arbeitsmarkt – Empirische Analyse und Reformansätze*, 1. Aufl., Baden-Baden: Nomos.

Streeck, W. (1994), European Social Policy after Maastricht: The Social Dialogue and Subsidarity; in: *Economic and Industrial Democracy*, Vol. 15, No 3, pp.151–178.

Streeck, W., Vitols, S. (1993), European Works Councils: Between Statutory Enactment and Voluntary Adoption; Berlin: WZB discussion paper FS 1 93–312.

Traxler, F., Kittel, B., Lengauer, S. (1996), Tarifsystem und Wettbewerbsfähigkeit; in: *Österreichische Zeitschrift für Sozialforschung*, Sonderband 3: Vernetzung und Vereinnahmung, pp.81–103, Opladen: Westdeutscher Verlag.

van den Berg, H., van der Veer, K. (1996), Tailor-made–Arbeitsvermittlung nach Mass; in: *Österreichische Zeitschrift für Soziologie*, 21. Jahrgang, Heft 3/1996, pp.6–29.

van Rijt, C. (1995), *Flexibilisering van de arbeid: een opiniepeiling onder het FNV-ledenpanel*; Amsterdam: Universiteit van Amsterdam/CESAR, November.

Vikklund, B. (1996), Sweden: Centralized Collective Bargaining without Government Influence; in: *Työelämän tutkimus*, Vol. 7, No 4, pp.5–10.

Walwei, U. (1996), Arbeitsvermittlung als öffentliche Aufgabe und privatwirtschaftliche Dienstleistung. Reorganization der Arbeitsvermittlung aus einer international vergleichenden Perspektive; in: *Mitteilungen aus der Arbeitsmarkt- und Berufsforschung*, Jg. 29, H. 1, pp.54–72.

Weinkopf, C. (1996), *Arbeitskräftepools. Überbetriebliche Beschäftigung im Spannungsfeld von Flexibilität, Mobilität und sozialer Sicherheit*, München und Mering: Rainer Hampp Verlag.

Weinkopf, C., (1996a), Dienstleistungspools – ein Ansatz zur Professionalisierung von Dienstleistungen in Privathaushalten? In: *WSI-Mitteilungen*, Jg. 49, H. 1, pp.36–43.

Weinkopf, C., Krone, S. (1995), START Zeitarbeit. Erste Erfahrungen und konzeptionelle überlegungen zum Einsatz sozialverträglicher Arbeitnehmerüberlassung als arbeitsmarkt-politisches Instrument, Gelsenkirchen: Ministerium für Arbeit, Gesundheit und Soziales des Landes Nordrhein-Westfalen.

White, M. (ed.) (1994), *Unemployment and Public Policy in a Changing Labour Market*; London: PSI.

Whitley, R. (1992), *European Business Systems: Firms and Markets in their National Context*; London: Sage.

Wilthagen, T. (1997), The concept of Flexicurity: Its role in the Dutch Labour Market Policy Reform and its relevance to a Theory of Transitional Labour Markets; Paper presented at the Research Unit Labour Market Policy and Employment of the Social Science Centre Berlin (WZB) on 2nd July.

Windhoff-Heritier, A. (1993), Wohlfahrtsstaatliche Interventionen im internationalen Vergleich Deutschland – Grossbritannien. Regulative Sozialpolitik am Beispiel des Arbeitsschutzes; in: *Leviathan (1993)*, No 1, pp.103–126.

Zanders, H., Koerhuis, C. (1997), *Working Time Flexibility in the Netherlands*, mimeo.

3.4. THE EMERGENCE OF NEW FORMS OF PROFESSIONAL CONDUCT AND NEW STRUCTURES OF WORK IN LOCAL DEVELOPMENT AND EMPLOYMENT INITIATIVES

Summary of the study conducted by Isabelle Perguilhem and Laurent Gardin with the assistance of Jacques Gautrat, Centre de recherche et d'information sur la démocratie et l'autonomie – CRIDA – with the assistance of the Laboratoire de sociologie du changement des institutions – LSCI / CNRS (French National Research Centre)

The White Paper on Growth, Competitiveness and Employment, which set out possible scenarios regarding employment in the European Union, attempted to respond to new needs arising from changes in lifestyle and family structures, the increase in the number of women in work and the ageing population.[44] To obtain a clearer understanding of the nature and extent of the phenomenon at European level, Commission departments carried out a study and published three working documents on local development and employment initiatives in 1995, 1997 and 1998.[45] They confirmed that local initiatives are flourishing in Europe and identified 19 fields of activity under four major headings:

- everyday services;
- services to improve the quality of life;
- cultural and leisure services;
- environmental services.

However, two questions need to be addressed: local development and employment initiatives generate socio-economic innovation by reason of their inception and their consolidating function, but can they also offer useful insights for the wider debate concerning the future of work? Are local development and employment initiatives examples of a new model where business follows employment? By analysing the reports on the work carried out in the cases of seven British and French local initiatives,[46]

---

[44] European Commission, White Paper on *Growth, Competition and Employment*, Luxembourg 1993.

[45] European Commission, *Local development and employment initiatives, European Union Survey*, Brussels, March 1995.

European Commission, First report on local development and employment initiatives – *Lessons for territorial and local pacts*, Directorate-General for Employment, Industrial Relations and Social Affairs, Brussels, November 1996.

European Commission, Second report on local development and employment initiatives – *The era of tailor-made jobs*, Brussels, January 1998

[46] CRIDA, *L'émergence de nouveaux comportements professionnels et de nouvelles organisations du travail dans les domaines d'ILDE*, January 1998.

the study set out to discover whether, possibly unwittingly, they introduced new practices reflecting theories on the emergence of post-industrial societies and the end of the time when work is the dominant factor in life.

Innovation was expected in the definition, planning and supervision of work. The aim was to identify the nature of flexibility in local initiatives needed in terms of weekly time-management, pay, differences in contracts and autonomy. It was also necessary to clarify the various participants' perceptions of work: would these initiatives reveal actors implementing complex strategies to meet their needs, by, for example, juggling 'activity portfolios' involving a mixture of salaried work, self-employed work, voluntary work and grants?

The main lesson to be learned from this study is that local development and employment initiatives do not fit neatly into a single theoretical category. They do not offer a counter-model, being a highly specific phenomenon where none of the standard concepts of salaried work apply.

3.4.1. The desire for normality as regards the employment contract

The initiatives do not focus on making work more flexible; they attempt to provide employees with security by means of standard full-time, open-ended contracts of paid employment. The contracts and periods of employment are similar, a fact reflected in

All the initiatives studied have been in existence for over three years and employ at least 20 people. They operate in various fields: home help, waste disposal, improving living conditions, the creation of groups of employers in rural areas, child-minding.

They are: INNOV'ENFANCE (Lille); ETRE (Caen); REGIE DE-QUARTIER (Orléans); APER (Poitou-Charente); TRIALP-VALESPACE (Chambéry); WALSALL HOME CARE CO-OPERATIVE (Walsall); WISE GROUP (Glasgow).

relatively small pay differentials (1 to 3). Local initiatives are therefore not sanctuaries for arranging how best to spend one's time or developing flexible careers: the attempts to structure fields where relatively menial jobs are rather common suggest that project organizers reject any form of atypical employment. Even where associations deploy home helps but do not employ the helps themselves, they reject the idea of self-employed work; although the home-helps are formally employed by the users, they are part of a working team managed by the organization. Far from inventing new work regulations, local development and employment initiatives place a high value on salaried work and the security it offers.

The study must not overlook the emphasis placed on contractual protection (collective agreements, for example, sufficient working hours to entitle staff to social rights, minimum wage, staff representation). The autonomy and commitment to the project sought by the local development and employment initiative operators are intended to enable their employees to gain a collective understanding of their work: if commitment is to enjoy more than mere lip-service, it must be based on solid foundations, involving proper pay and enforceability of the contract under ordinary law. This is one of the key concerns for permanent local development and employment initiatives, which refuse to see themselves simply as cobbled-together integration experiments to compensate for the shortcomings of the market. They do not work on the basis of fixed-term job-creation contracts; the aim is to create sustainable jobs to limit the risk of being exploited by public policies to counter the social impact of unemployment. It must be pointed out here that some French home help and child-minding initiatives have encountered difficulties owing to the absence of standard regulations. Home-help service providers are unwilling to be viewed as domestic employees, while pay for home carers remains low because the lack of a national framework has resulted in financial partners continuing to view them as glorified baby-sitters. Local development and employment initiatives do more than just provide protection through social welfare measures; for example, there is also a link with national collective bargaining to lend a higher profile to the jobs created.

Local development and employment initiatives, then, cannot be viewed as a method of employing sections of the population which are permanently excluded from traditional employment or as a closed tertiary sector where full-time salaried staff play a minimal role in comparison with voluntary or self-employed work.

The pursuit of normality must not be overlooked, as local development and employment initiatives often operate in low-status fields. The attempt to structure supply and to regulate the form of employment is in itself innovative. It also makes it easier to link up with voluntary work, which is another characteristic of these organizations.

3.4.2. The relationship between paid and voluntary work

Local development and employment initiatives extend their 'catchment area' to include voluntary workers, who can fulfil several functions. In some cases voluntary work provides specific support for certain events. For example, an initiative to maintain local areas wanted to organize an annual competition for the best balcony garden in the district. This type of voluntary work had never been done before; the local development and employment initiative created the opportunity in their area.

Voluntary work can also, though less often, play a long-term role in the provision of services. There is no problem with linking voluntary and salaried work, as long as the two sectors perform different functions.

The most common case of voluntary-workers' involvement is that of sitting on local development and employment initiative decision-making bodies. Within these bodies, partnership is fostered and environmental and strategy questions are addressed. Of course, this is a means of consolidating the management structure, but also of checking that the basic project's societal objectives are attained.

The inclusion of voluntary work by local development and employment initiatives is not viewed as a threat because paid work is protected and acknowledged. By the same token, whether voluntary work is performed by users or the rank and file, it does not replace paid work. On the contrary, it may increase the number of opportunities for employment by reducing the cost price and facilitating the close permanent links between users and other local partners. This use of voice rather than exit[47] is particularly valuable in relation to personal services because it enables quality criteria to be developed by means of a three-way negotiation between service providers, voluntary workers and users.

3.4.3. The relationship between users and professional attitudes

One of the general features of local development and employment initiatives is that priority tends to be given to services in economic activities. However, while there is a consensus that in the future job-creation will be concentrated in the tertiary sector, it should be pointed out that the services in question are relatively independent of the industrial system and the manufacturing sector in that they are relational services. Relational services are defined as services based on direct interaction between the service provider and the user, due either to the nature of the activity, as in the field of health care, or to the choice of the method of implementation, as in cases of environmental protection , where the objective is to raise public awareness.

---

[47] To use the categories developed by A.O. Hirschman: voice and exit; in: *Face au déclin des entreprises et des institutions*, Les Editions Ouvrières, Paris 1972.

Local initiatives are innovative in terms of the nature of the relationship they develop with users. Users are represented in the structure (on the management board) and are involved in the definition of the service and the strategic guidelines of the initiatives. They are seen as partners rather than clients. Consequently, they do not play the part of consumers acting solely on the basis of their financial power (to purchase or not); they participate actively in the project.

On the basis of this relationship with users, local development and employment initiatives tend to invert the argument that initial qualification is a pre-requisite for career prospects. They gamble on the fact that, once people have found work, they will then acquire the necessary skills. The necessary skills go beyond the ability to work in a team or get on well with clients; they are closely linked to an involvement in the project. Where personal services are involved, apart from the practical tasks, the participants must be helped to develop a relationship of interdependence without dominating or being dominated. To achieve this, the organizations develop a wide range of training possibilities, from workshops and tutorials to discussion and support facilities. On the basis of this relational proximity which underlies the occupational framework, the local development and employment initiatives succeed in developing real tailor-made programmes based around collective projects. At this point the initiatives can be opened up to discussion and negotiation regarding the original project and enabling practical professional behaviour to emerge.

These values are not the driving force behind the local development and employment initiatives; they are the outcome of their day-to-day workings. In most cases, the idea of a collective common good basically originates with the support group, the project organizer and, to a lesser extent, the management team. The setting up of the initiative reflects their societal aspirations. They find a purpose by entering into a publicly minded spirit, as voluntary workers on some management boards have said. However, looking at all the teams, we have not set up a 'third-way' organizational form shaped by a set of constant values. We have seen instead that the structures are anchored in their local areas, with varying degrees of flexibility, where most staff, when talking about work, mention the security of an unlimited full-time contract. Most but not all. By emphasising the relationship aspect of the service being provided, some local development and employment initiatives stimulate in some of their paid workers forms of motivation which cannot be reduced to mere financial security, such as autonomy, opportunities to take the initiative and try out new ideas, or an awareness of the impact of their work on users and the group as a whole. Therefore the close relationship with users maximizes the sense of responsibility among paid workers, which means developing the content of their work to shape the service being provided. Thus, work in the initiative must provide the possibility for self-expression and recognition by the organization as a genuine human resource.

If local development and employment initiatives are seen as an expression of post-industrial society, this is less a function of their rejection of pay or post-war capitalist structures than a consequence of the way they create an economy on a human level, with citizens making a contribution to local life rather than consumers and producers interacting in the traditional sense.

Local initiatives raise the problem of the relationship between voluntary and paid work. The idea is not to consolidate workfare, where there is an obligation to work in fields deemed to be socially useful in exchange for state benefits, or to invent regulations shifting the work into the specific area of local services. It is to develop systems that involve various parties. The characteristic feature is not just that the two types of work co-exist; the users also have a recognized role.

3.4.4. Bibliography

Afriat, C., Caspar, P. (1988), L'investissement intellectuel, Essai sur l'économie de l'immatériel; in: *Economica*, Paris.

Anspach, M.R. (1996), L'archipel du Welfare américain, âge d'abondance, âge de pierre; in: *Revue du Mauss, Vers un revenu minimum inconditionnel?*, No 7, first quarter.

Anxo, D., Boulin, J.Y., Lallement, M., Lefèvre, G., Silvera, R. (1997)**,** *Partage du travail et mode de vie des salariés, comparaison France-Suède*, SET-METIS, CNRS, Paris I, Mimeograph, October.

Arendt, A.H (1983), *Condition de l'homme moderne* (French translation), Paris, Calmann-Lévy.

Audrey (1994), *Le travail après la crise*, Interéditions, Paris.

Auer, P. (1990), Emploi, marché du travail et stratégies de lutte contre le chômage; in: *Chroniques internationales du marché du travail et des politiques de l'emploi 1986-1989*. Paris: La Documentation Française, Paris.

Baumol, W.J. (1987), Microeconomics of Unbalanced Growth: The Anatomy of the Urban Crisis; in: *American Economic Review*, June.

Ben Ner, A., Van Hoomissen, T. (1991)**,** *Non Profit Organizations in the Mixed Economy, Annals of Public and Co-operative Economy*, Vol. 4.

Borzaga, C., Santuari, A. (dir.) (1998), *Social Enterprises and New Employment in Europe*, Trentino, in co-operation with European Commision-DGV, CGM-Consorzio nazionale della cooperazione sociale.

Bridges, W. (1995), in: *La conquête du travail: au-delà des transitions*, Village Mondial, Paris.

Caillé, A., Laville, J.L. (ed.) (1998), Une seule solution, l'association? Socio-économie du fait associatif; in: *La Revue du MAUSS*, (a bi-annual publication), No 11, first half.

Castel, R., Lae, J.F. (1992), La diagonale du pauvre; in: Castel, R., Lae, J.F., *Le revenu minimum d'insertion. Une dette sociale*, Paris, Editions de l'Harmattan.

Castel, R., Schnapper, D. (1994), 'Non, le travail ce n'est pas fini'; in: *Libération*, 24 June.

Castel, R. (1995), Chapitre VII: La société salariale; in: *Les métamorphoses de la question sociale*, Paris, Fayard.

Castel, R. (1995), À propos de la fin du travail salarié de William Bridges; in: *Partage*, a weekly information publication on unemployment and work, No 96, April.

Chateauraynaud, F., Choquet, L.H. (1991), Enquête sur les archives administratives du RMI. Note No 2: ligne du contrat d'insertion, CEE (European Economic Community), mimeograph, April.

Combemale, P. (1987), *INSEE Ecoflash*, 22 October.

Conseil Supérieur de l'Emploi, des Revenus et des Coûts (CSERC) (1996), L'allégement des charges sociales sur les bas salaires, Rapport au Premier ministre (Report to the Prime Minister), Paris.

Conseil Supérieur de l'Emploi, des Revenus et des Coûts (CSERC) (1997), *Minima sociaux, entre protection et insertion*, Paris, La Documentation Française.

Council of Economic Advisors (1995), Annual Report.

Coutrot (1997), La réduction du temps de travail: mesure technocratique ou innovation conflictuelle? In: '*Appel des économistes pour sortir de la pensée unique*', Pour un nouveau plein emploi, Syros, Paris.

de Jouvenel, H. (1995), La société française à l'horizon 2010: réinventer l'univers du travail; in: *Le travail au XXIème siècle*, Dunod, Paris.

de Tocqueville, A. (1961), *De la démocratie en Amérique*, Vol. 2, Gallimard, Paris

Defalvard, H., Guienne, V. (ed.) (1998), *Le partage du travail*, Desclée de Brouwer, Paris.

Dent, H. (1995), *Job Choc*, First Éditions, Paris.

Donzelot, J., Jaillet, M.C. (1997), Europe, Etats-Unis: convergences et divergences des politiques d'insertion; in: *Esprit* magazine.

Drin, L. (1998), *La société française en tendances 1975–1995*, Chapter V-13: Affaiblissement des grands conflits idéologiques et montée d'un sentiment de mal-être, Chapter V-14: Développement de signes d'anomie, Paris, Presses Universitaires de France.

Du Tertre, C. (1995), Le changement du travail et de l'emploi: le rôle majeur des 'relations de service'; in: *Les Cahiers de Syndex*, No 4.

Dubar, C. (1991), *La socialisation. Construction des identités sociales et professionnelle*, Paris, Armand Colin.

Dumazedier, J. (1988), *La révolution culturelle du temps libre, 1948–1988*, Paris: Méridiens-Kliencsieck.

Duval, G. (1998), 'L'ère des entreprises-réseaux'; in: *Alternatives économiques*, No 162, September.

Elbaum, M. (1994), Les activités intermédiaires: une sphère d'insertion 'autonome' et un mode de partage du travail 'par défaut'; in: *Travail et emploi*, October.

Eme, B. (1994), Insertion et économie solidaire; in: Eme, B., Laville, J.L. *Cohésion sociale et emploi*, Desclée de Brouwer.

Eme, B., Laville, J.L. (sous la direction) (1994), *Cohésion sociale et emploi*, Desclée de Brouwer, Paris.

Eme, B., Laville, J.L. (1996), L'intégration sociale entre conditionnalité et inconditionnalité; in: *Revue française des affaires sociales*, No 3.96.

Esping-Andersen, Gosta (1990), *The Three Worlds of Welfare Capitalism*, Princetown University Press, Princetown.

European Commission (1995), *The local development and employment initiatives*, Survey in the European Union, March.

European Commission (1996), *First report on local development and employment initiatives*, European Community, Luxembourg.

Favrot-Laurens, G. (1996), Culture domestique et pratiques de délégation, research for the Construction-Architecture Plan, Toulouse.

Ferry, J.M. (1995), *L'Allocation universelle*, Paris: Les Éditions du Cerf.

Frémeaux, P., Maurin, L. (1996), Emploi, le grand contresens; in: *Alternatives Économiques*, No 135, March.

Freyssinet, J. (1989), *Les mécanismes de création-destruction d'emplois*, Paris, IRES (mimeograph).

Gadrey, J. (1997), Croissance ou partage? Deux logiques à réconcilier; in: *'Appel des économistes pour sortir de la pensée unique', Pour un nouveau plein emploi*, Syros, Paris.

Gadrey, J., Jany-Catrice, F. (1998), Créer plus d'un million d'emplois dans le commerce de détail par la baisse des charges sociales en s'inspirant du modèle américain? L'erreur économique, working paper of the Appel des Économistes pour sortir de la Pensée Unique ('Call by economists to go beyond the one-track thinking'), February 1998 (paper published by *Partage*, No 124, July–August, 1998.)

Gaullier, X. (1995), Quel avenir pour les quinquagénaires? In: *Le Monde*, May 24.

Godbout, J., Caillé, A. (1992), L'esprit du don, *La Découverte*, Paris, p.197.

Godet, M. (1994), *Emploi: le grand mensonge*, Éditions Fixot, Paris.

Gorz, A. (1988), *Métamorphoses du travail. Quête du sens*, Paris, Editions Galilée.

Gorz, A. (1995), Mutation technique et changement culturel; in: *Échange et Projets*, No 73, February.

Gorz, A. (1995), A propos de l'utopie ultra-libérale de Bridges: Re-Engineering; in: *Partage*, No 96, April.

Greffe, X. ed. (1990), *Nouvelles demandes, nouveaux services*, Commissariat Général du Plan, Paris, La Documentation Française.

Grozelier, A.M. (1998), *Pour en finir avec la fin du travail*, Les Éditions de l'Atelier, Paris.

Guggenberger, B. (1988), *Wenn uns die Arbeit ausgeht*, Hanser.

Handy, C. (1995), *Le temps des paradoxes*, Village Mondial, Paris.

Heclo, H. (1974), *Modern Social Politics in Britain and Sweden*, Yale University Press, New Haven – London.

Hirata, S., Senotier, D (ed.) (1996), *Femmes et partage du travail*, Syros, Paris.

Hoang-Ngoc, L. (1997), Existe-t-il une 'autre politique' pour sortir de l'impasse libérale? In: *'Appel des économistes pour sortir de la pensée unique', Pour un nouveau plein emploi*, Syros, Paris.

INSEE Première (1992), *La montée du temps partiel*, No 237, December.

Jones, C. (1993), *New Perspectives on the Welfare States in Europe*, Routledge, London.

Juan, S. (1997), Les segmentations symboliques instituées et vécues; in: Gauthier (ed.) *Aux frontières du social: l'exclu*, Harmattan, Paris.

Kaufmann, J.C. (1996), *Faire ou faire-faire? Familles et services*, Rennes, Presses Universitaires de Rennes.

Kosistimen, B., Nieminen, A. (1997), *Sociological Literature on the Future of Work*, University of Tampere.

Krugman, P. (1995), L'Europe sans emploi, l'Amérique sans le sou? In: *Futuribles*, September (translation of article in *Foreign Policy*, summer 1994).

Lallement, M. (1994), 'L'État et l'emploi'; in: Eme, B., Laville, J.L., *Cohésion sociale et emploi*, Desclée de Brouwer, Paris.

Landier, H. (1995), Le syndicalisme à réinventer; in: *Sociétal*, No 1; for further details, see his book, *Dessine-moi une vie active*, Village Mondial, Paris.

Laville, J.L. (ed.) (1992), *Les services de proximité en Europe*. Paris, Syros-Alternatives.

Laville, J.L. (ed.) (1996), *L'économie solidaire. Une perspective internationale*, Desclée de Brouwer, Paris.

Laville, J.L. (1997), 'Le renouveau de la sociologie économique'; in: *Cahiers Internationaux de Sociologie*, Vol. CIII – Sociologies économiques, Presses universitaires de France, July–December.

Laville, J.L. (1998), Associations et activités économiques: l'exemple des services de proximité; in: *La Revue du MAUSS*, (published twice-yearly), Une seule solution, l'association? Socio-économie du fait associatif, No 11, 1st half.

Lebaube, A. (1987), *L'emploi en miettes*, Paris: Hachette.

Lefresne, F. (1997), 'Politique de l'emploi: les vrais enjeux du débat sur son efficacité'; in: *'Appel des économistes pour sortir de la pensée unique', Pour un nouveau plein emploi,* Syros, Paris.

Le Monde (1995), *'Les contrats emploi-solidarité débouchent rarement sur un travail',* March 27.

Letablier, M.T. (1996), *Emploi-famille: des ajustements variables selon les pays,* Lettre du Centre d'études de l'emploi, No 37, April.

Lipietz, A. (1996), *La société en sablier,* La Découverte, Paris.

Lojkine, J. (1992), *La révolution informationnelle,* Presses universitaires de France, Paris.

Majnoni d'Intignano, B. (1998), *L'usine à chômeurs,* Plon, Paris

Malinvaud, E. (1986), Sur les statistiques de l'emploi et du chômage, *Report to the Prime Minister,* Paris: La Documentation Française.

Maruani, M. (1994), *Temps, emplois, revenus: anciens clivages, nouveaux partages,* CSU-CNRS, Colloque 'Familles et recherches', IDEF, Paris.

Maruani, M. (1994), Marché du travail et marchandage social; in: Lallement, M. (ed.), *Travail et emploi. Le temps des métamorphoses,* Paris: L'Harmattan.

Maurin, L. (1995), Le temps partiel ou la réduction du temps de travail version entreprises; in: *Alternatives Économiques,* No 128, June.

Méda, D. (1995), *Le travail. Une valeur en voie de disparition,* Aubier, Paris.

Méda, D. (1997), 'Travail, emploi, activité: des redéfinitions en cours', paper delivered at the conference: 'Travail, activité, emploi: formes, rythmes et règles. Une comparaison France-Allemagne'. Paris, Ministère de l'emploi et de la solidarité, 9 et 10 October.

Ministère du travail, de l'emploi et de la formation professionnelle (1993), *Nouveaux services, nouveaux emplois,* Paris, La Documentation Française.

Morin, M.L. (1997), in the conclusion to his research based on empirical analysis; in: Morin, M.L. (ed.), *Prestation du travail et*

activité de service, Laboratoire interdisciplinaire de recherche sur les resources humaines et l'emploi, Toulouse.

Mothé, D. (1998), *L'utopie du temps libre,* Éditions Esprit, Paris.

Nyssens, M., Petrella, F. (1996), L'organisation des services de proximité à Charleroi: vers une économie plurielle? In: *Les cahiers du CERISIS,* 96/1. Centre de Recherche Interdisciplinaire pour la Solidarité et l'Innovation Sociale (CERISIS) – Hainaut, UCL.

OECD (1995), *L'étude de l'OCDE sur l'emploi,* Paris.

Passet, R. (1995), Les voies d'une économie plurielle; Transversales Sciences Culture (special issue); in: *L'Alternative,* 32, March–April.

Paysant, M. (1995), *Travail salarié – travail indépendant,* Flammarion, Paris.

Perez, C. (forthcoming), La 'politique publique d'emploi' américaine; in: Barbier, J.C., Gautié, J.J. (ed.), *Les politiques d'emploi.*

Perguilhem, I. (1998), *L'émergence de nouvelles organisations du travail et de nouveaux comportements professionnels dans les initiatives locales de développement et d'emploi,* CRIDA-LSCI, CNRS.

Perret, B. (1995), *L'avenir du travail,* Paris, Le Seuil.

Perret, B., Roustang, G. (1993), *L'économie contre la société,* Seuil, Paris.

Perrot, M. (1993), *Vendredi-Idées,* June.

Petit, P. (1988), *La croissance tertiaire,* Économica, Paris.

Piketty, T. (1997), Les créations d'emplois en France et aux États-Unis, 'services de proximité' contre petits boulots'?, Notes de la Fondation Saint-Simon, No 93, December, Paris.

Pretot, X. (1990), 'Le droit à l'insertion'; in: Alfanderi, E. (ed.), *L'insertion,* Paris, Sirey.

Putnam, R.D. (1993), *Making Democracy Work: Civil Traditions in Modern Italy,* Princeton, Princeton University Press.

Robin, J. (1993), *Quand le travail quitte la société post-industrielle,* Vol. 1, Paris: GRIT éditeurs.

Rosanvallon, P. (1995), *La nouvelle question sociale. Repenser l'Etat-providence,* Paris: Le Seuil.

Roustang, G. (1987), *L'emploi: un choix de société*, Paris: Syros.

Roustang, G. (1997), *De la politique économique à l'anthropologie économique*, mimeograph, CNRS-Laboratoire d'économie et de sociologie du travail, Aix-en-Provence.

Roustang, G. (1997), 'A propos de 'la fin du travail' de Jeremy Rifkin. Vers un nouveau contrat social'; in: *Partage*, No 110, January.

Roustang, G., Laville, J.L., Eme, B., Mothé, D., Perret, B. (1997), *Vers un nouveau contrat social*, Desclée de Brouwer, Paris.

Sainsaulieu, R. (1977), *L'identité au travail*, Presses de la Fondation Nationale des Sciences Politiques, Paris.

Sauvy, A. (1980), *La machine et le chômage*, Dunod, Paris.

Schnapper, D. (1997), *Contre la fin du travail*, Textuel, Paris.

Schumpeter, J. (1941), *Capitalisme, socialisme et démocratie* (French translation), Payot, Paris.

Simmel, G. (1987), *Philosophie de l'argent*, Presses universitaires de France, Paris, (French translation).

Strobel, P. (1995), Service public, fin de siècle; in: Gremion, C. (ed.), *Modernisation des services publics*, Commissariat général du plan, Ministère de la recherche, La Documentation Française, Paris.

Sue, R. (1997), *La richesse des hommes*, Editions Odile Jacob.

Touraine, A. (1978), *La voix et le regard*, Le Seuil, Paris.

Veltz, P. (1998), *'La mondialisation: de quoi parle-t-on?'*, Etudes pour une région, Région Nord-Pas de Calais, Conseil régional, No 2, January.

Walzer, M (1995), Individus et communautés: les deux pluralismes; in: *Esprit*, 6, juin.

Wenz-Dumas, F. (1993), Les jeunes stationnent dans la zone grise du travail; in: *Libération*, September 15.

Wilson, W.J. (1987), *The Truly Disadvantaged. The Inner City, the Underclass and Public Policy*, University of Chicago Press.

Wuhl, S. (1994), 'Quelle politique d'insertion pour quel chômage'; in: *Esprit*, 12, December.

123

Part II

When European civil society debates work: Results of the European Social Forum 24–26 June 1998

Launched in 1996, the European Social Policy Forum brings together, every two years, representatives of civil society and government bodies in order to take forward the process of debate and reflection on the social dimension of European integration. One of the three themes chosen for the workshops at the 1998 session was that of the 'future world of work'. Drawing on a preliminary report produced by P. Townsend,[48] the workshop involved a number of different speakers with around one hundred people taking part.

The main conclusions were then presented for general discussion, which enriched the debate. Overall, the event bore witness to the vitality of those active in this field, whose thinking and whose proposals are firmly rooted in practice and an understanding of human beings, and should thus provide inspiration for the European project.

---

[48] Rapporteur for the Forum.

We have endeavoured to reconstruct the main themes of the debate, looking forward to possible consensus on the future of work in Europe. Such a consensus presupposes, as we will see, greater convergence of attitudes to work and the economy.

Chapter 4

The social challenge for Europe

First of all, the debate attempted to outline the challenges of European integration, examining them in the light of current economic and labour market trends, in order to compare them with employment policy as it is actually practised.

4.1. TRENDS: UNEMPLOYMENT AND INEQUALITIES

Overall, Europe's economy is prospering. It is performing well in the face of globalization and the development of information technology. As regards the issue of work, however, it shows at least two major shortcomings:

- *The economy is not creating enough jobs, given the growth in the working population*
  The population of working age (15 to 64 years) grew from 207 to 246 million people between 1975 and 1996, and the number of jobless from 13.3 to 14.8 million. Contrary to what is sometimes asserted, we are not experiencing jobless growth (growth of 2 per cent is sufficient to create jobs, as opposed to 4 per cent formerly). However, the 'overspill'[49] (dear to

---

[49] Dunod, *La machine et le chômage*, 1980.

A. Sauvy) into new sectors of activity is not taking place as easily as in the United States, while the working population has increased considerably under the combined effect of the post-war 'baby boom' and the mass entry of women into the labour market.

- *Growth is increasingly polarized and unequal*
  The number of people living below the poverty line grew from 49 to 61 million between 1980 and 1988. According to the International Labour Organisation (ILO), the real income of workers on low salaries has even fallen in some countries, not only in relative terms but also in absolute terms. This trend varies from country to country; the Nordic countries are less affected than the United Kingdom at the other extreme. It highlights the phenomenon of social polarization, which is gaining ground across Europe, under the influence of growing unemployment (including long-term unemployment) and, more fundamentally, a type of economic development which tends to place work on a precarious footing (fixed-term contracts, temporary contracts, part-time work) and to put low-skilled workers at a disadvantage. Women, older workers, disabled workers and ethnic minorities are also victims of a discrimination, which is particularly marked on the labour market.

In the long run, such growth 'benefits the winners': so what is to be done with all those who do not find their place in the world of work or who do not find a worthwhile job which is within their capabilities?

4.2. THE CHALLENGES: AN ACTIVE AND MUTUALLY SUPPORTIVE SOCIETY

There are two main responses to the changes affecting the world of work. Such was the essential message from the non-governmental organizations (NGOs). For some, these changes represent the 'end of work' or, rather, the end of work as a job which in itself guarantees income, status and social ties. This justifies the preparation of a new social contract and a citizen's income not linked to work. For others, these changes constitute new challenges with regard to the distribution of paid work and of income, requiring a recommitment to full employment.

Although the first approach is not without practical interest, in particular since it highlights the need to take better account of unpaid work, most participants rejected it none the less. They consider paid work to be essential in our society, not only as a means of earning an income but, more fundamentally, as a foundation for identity and social ties. European civil society calls for an 'active society'[50] in which everyone can develop skills and live a dignified life thanks to work. Consequently, the majority wishes to see an economy with full employment, though some qualify this approach by reducing the relative importance of paid work (notably by reducing working time and focusing on the role of unpaid work).

Likewise, society must show *solidarity*. This dual obligation precludes the straightforward adoption of the American model, where it is possible for everyone to be 'active', but in ways that do not appear compatible with European society. Consequently, we need to find ways of *sharing both work and income* (the mere sharing of work could be very unequal) and of developing equal opportunities (between men and women especially, but also to benefit low-skilled workers), taking care not to disconnect the 'employment' and 'poverty' dimensions (some employment policies can aggravate poverty, as ATD Quart Monde stressed). We need to build a 'Europe for all', in the words of President Santer. But is this really the inspiration behind the European Union's current policy?

---

[50] A concept invented some years ago by Ron Gass, Director for Social Affairs at the OECD.

4.3. A MUCH DEBATED POLICY

The European Union is not only economic and monetary. It has started to introduce a social dimension which, as Commissioner Flynn emphasized, must become a foundation stone of European integration, and not simply one of its consequences. The intention to make it so was translated into action quite recently with the adoption of a European Employment Strategy in the context of the Amsterdam Treaty (June 1997) and at the Luxembourg summit (November 1997); Member States have been given greater responsibility, common objectives have been set for employment and a convergence process has been launched, involving a multi-annual surveillance mechanism.

Building on the macro-economic stability furthered by the Maastricht Treaty, the Employment Strategy adopted at Cardiff (June 1998) calls for an integrated and synchronized approach based around four pillars of action:

- improving the employability of the unemployed;
- developing entrepreneurship;
- promoting the adaptability of workers and firms;
- promoting equal opportunities.

While the participants, along with the Commissioner, welcomed this recent impetus for a common employment policy in Europe, they none the less expressed a number of reservations.

The first concerns the *need to link*, as mentioned above, the *issues of employment and poverty.* The NGOs regret that the Luxembourg agreement did not link the objective of job creation to that of reducing poverty. In their view, it is necessary to promote decent jobs, which are accessible to the poorest people, and not jobs at any price. With this in mind, more appropriate convergence indicators should be used.

The second reservation, which was naturally not shared by the employers' representatives, highlighted the *excessive importance placed on the need for competitiveness.* Adjustment to change (watchword of the European Commission) is called into question: where will change lead? Should we accept, for the sake of employment and competitiveness, an ever-increasing pressure on employees, likening them, as one participant did, to high-speed trains? This criticism echoes that made of globalization, which, while it should not be demonized, should be controlled so that it can be put to the service of people and not transnational firms. The current concern of the European Union, however, – and in this it represents its members – seems to be to keep on top of international competition by submitting to its rules, instead of questioning them. Given its weight and its economic and monetary union, would it not be within Europe's power to act differently?

Lastly, the strongest criticism was directed at the *marginal role given to employment policy*, as compared with economic policy. In the view of most participants, we are still a long way from a situation where the social dimension is at the heart of the European model, to borrow the phrase used by Mr Blunkett, UK Secretary of State, in his contribution to the Forum. Is the social dimension just a variable to be adjusted, or the necessary complement to economic and monetary union, its only purpose being to prevent social dumping? Several participants highlighted the contradiction between a balanced budget policy and the recently introduced social dimension of Europe. 'Should we not launch a debate on the necessity or otherwise of limiting tax and social security contributions?' was a question put by the NGO representative. What should be done to ensure that the European Stability Pact[51] is seen as an asset which can boost the economy,

---

[51] The Stability and Growth Pact is part of the third stage of economic and monetary union. It is intended to ensure that Member States continue to pursue budgetary discipline after the introduction of the single currency. It takes the form of a Resolution of the European Council (adopted at Amsterdam on 17 June 1997) and two Council Regulations (7 July 1997) on the practical implementing arrangements.

whereas at present, in the view of the representative of the European Trade Union Confederation, it acts against employment? All these questions highlight the different conceptions of economic and social issues found in Europe.

Chapter 5

Plural conceptions

Before outlining the many proposals that came out of the debate, it is useful to summarize the conceptions that Europeans have of work and the economy. These conceptions play a key role in the implementation of policies which, as we will see further on, presuppose co-operation between the various players. However, although different conceptions are held by employers, unions and NGOs, it emerged clearly from the discussions that they are not necessarily irreconcilable but in fact complementary. There is a plurality of conceptions that can mutually strengthen, rather than oppose, one another (see below, the concept of a 'plural economy'). It therefore seems possible today to reach a certain consensus starting from apparently divergent initial conceptions.

5.1. OF WORK

Beyond the horizon of paid work

The speculations of theoreticians about the end of work do not meet with much success among those involved on the ground, who consider that the priority is to ensure that everyone has access to a paid job. Divorcing work and income by introducing a universal allowance would not, according to D. Meulders,[52] be

---

[52] Economist, DULBEA, Université Libre de Bruxelles.

so advantageous in practice as the theoreticians believe and, to be realistic, would entail such complexity that it might well, in its turn, have numerous perverse effects. According to Professor Meulders, it would be wiser (as a first step?) to introduce a universal benefit system for children regardless of the status of their parents, their income or the size of the family.

Thus, the universal allowance meets with condemnation even as it partially re-enters the debate. The same applies to unpaid work. The participants in the Forum considered that the basis for social cohesion must remain paid work, but that we should find ways of enhancing the value of unpaid work, which accounts for 30 per cent to 40 per cent of gross domestic product (GDP) in many European countries.

As for work-sharing, in the sense of drastically reducing working time for everyone, it represents the meeting point between two concerns: providing paid work for everyone while at the same time reducing its relative importance. Work-sharing could also be a means of more easily reconciling family/community/ private life with one's career and thus promoting greater equality of opportunity between men and women. It is to be regretted that this subject was barely discussed, the French seeming rather isolated on this subject.

Can two concepts of flexibility be reconciled?

The demand for flexibility is a key characteristic of the changes affecting work. The demand comes both from employers, wishing to increase their firm's competitiveness, and from employees, wishing to combine work better with their other focuses of interest. At present, however, the notion of flexibility is associated more with deregulation and the increasing precariousness of the labour market. Several participants pointed out that this 'external' conception of flexibility (according to which the risks are borne by persons outside the firm) may, in the long term, have a negative effect on the productivity of the labour force, and that countries with highly regulated labour markets are not necessarily the least dynamic.

The opposite conception is that of 'internal' flexibility, which puts the emphasis on the firm's own responsibility for organising work and on the quality of life of the workers, who should be given guarantees as regards their status. In reality, even if flexibility is implemented at an exclusively internal level, it is likely to result in the exclusion of the least skilled because of the emphasis on relational skills, as stressed in the NGO document. Part-time work is also a very ambiguous term: it may be imposed but it may also be 'chosen time', a concept which was not in fact referred to during the debate.

The traditional views of employers and trade unions could not be fully reconciled on this point, but we none the less had the impression that their positions were not so distant from each other: the employers' representative recognized the need for regulating new types of work and called for 'flexibility', primarily for job creation and for small and medium-sized enterprises (SMEs). The employees' representatives did not contest the need for this.

At European level, if not at national level, it does not seem impossible that a compromise could be reached between these two positions, bearing in mind the attachment of both sides to certain values of the European social model. But can this compromise be maintained in the face of international competition, which is likely to get tougher? In other words, will Europe be strong and united enough to offer the world a more humane model of flexibility?

A job at any price?

Participants were almost unanimous in proclaiming the need for a 'working' society, but were divided on some of its consequences. The idea of 'activating' passive expenditure on unemployment could, for example, result in a form of 'forced labour', prefigured by the 'workfare' experiment in the Anglo-Saxon countries. The idea of offering everyone employment in socially useful activities could in its turn result in ghettos 'for the poor'. As to the development of personal services and to how they are to be paid for, this could result in a new kind of 'domestic service'. Lastly, as we have seen, offers of part-time work may give rise to shameless exploitation of certain categories of worker, especially women, who would end up facing even greater discrimination.

Let us not forget that work has two aspects: one is the 'creative' aspect, which allows each person to develop, and the other is the constraint (*'tripalium'*) which forces human beings to engage in toil. We should therefore be careful of blanket condemnations of the workfare experiment (which, in its British version, is not equivalent to forced labour) or of policies for making resources available for personal services (services which do not necessarily correspond to 'domestic service'), or of part-time work which, although not voluntary, may open the door to employment.

In other words, all these forms of activating employment present undeniable risks, but they may be worth introducing, if they are set up in such a way as to reduce poverty, with internal flexibility as the goal (so that part-time or fixed-term contracts form part of genuine career paths) and in accordance with ILO Convention 122[53] – to which attention was drawn by the NGOs: 'this policy must aim to ensure (. . .) freedom of choice as regards work'.

5.2. OF THE ECONOMY

Is there a 'real' economy?

As Professor Borzaga brilliantly demonstrated, one of the main job-creation methods which is compatible with the European

---

[53] International Labour Organisation Convention C122 on employment policy, 1964 (entered into force on 15 July 1966). For more information see: htpp://ilolex.ilo.ch:1567/scripts/

social model involves developing the 'social economy', i.e. non-profit-making economic entities combining commercial, public and voluntary resources. Other solutions are of course conceivable in the context of the (often latent) demand for personal and community services:

- First solution: increasing the public supply of services. However, this approach runs into difficulties with public funding, and it is not always suitable, given that demand is necessarily individualized;
- Second solution: developing wage flexibility on the American model. This feasibility of option is also limited, given European values;
- Third solution: creating a 'secondary' labour market for the unemployed. Most European countries have used and abused this option. But it has not been very fruitful: it has reduced the credibility of the new activities in question and locked the unemployed into cycles which, in too many cases, offer few real prospects.

A discussion took place on this subject between Ms T. De Liedekerke, the employers' representative, and C. Borzaga,[54] centring on the order of priority which should be established between these various options. For Ms De Liedekerke, all these solutions were worth considering, on condition that as many of the working population as possible remained on the 'real' labour market. Professor Borzaga was also in favour of a 'multi-pronged' approach but expressed the hope (as we will see further on) that the potential of the social economy would be better exploited.

At this point in the debate, a consensus was reached on a certain 'plurality' of economic activities. But is it just a question of 'tolerating' the unconventional economy, which can be financed only if the market economy is healthy and which, at the end of

---

[54] Carlo Borzaga is Professor of Economics at the University of Trento.

the day, constitutes a more subtle form of redistribution? Or should we think of the economy in a more systemic fashion (as F. Braudel[55] did in his own way), with the market economy itself dependent on apparently less 'complete' economic forms, which involve civil society and generate 'external savings'? The concept of a plural economy, it seems to us, should work both ways, reflecting the need for cross-fertilization between the economy based on competition and that based on social relations.[56]

In this context, the underground economy could be viewed, not – as is often the case – as an illegal economy to be penalized, but as a potential source of new jobs that the social economy could exploit.

In reality, as a number of participants pointed out, this debate about the 'real economy' is only one aspect of a wider debate between the economic and social worlds. The market economy has increasingly excluded the social dimension from its mode of operation. It was in this spirit (a 'common market') that the European Union was formed and primarily continues to operate, in particular by taking systematic action to increase the dominance and transparency of the market. Today, although we have recognized the need to reintroduce the social dimension, the latter is still outside the frame, especially as regards the conceptions we have of economic operation.

The social or 'mutually supportive' economy makes a breach in the wall, which divides economy and society and needs to be the subject of an essential debate. Too often the issues are obscured by discussions on growth.

---

[55] François-Xavier Verschave, *Civilisation matérielle, économie et capitalisme*, Libres leçons de Braudel, Syros 1995.

[56] Cf. Reconciling economy and society: *Towards a plural economy*, OECD paperback No 12, 1997.

What kind of growth?

The debate on this subject was more typical and legitimate, but rather second-rate. Most of the contributors called for more growth, but for some (employers), this meant 'clean' growth without any fiscal or monetary 'tricks', based on greater labour-market flexibility and the creation of enterprises. Others (trade unionists) saw the Maastricht criteria as being too rigid. Now that the single currency had been introduced, we should build on this stability to stimulate the economy.

Without calling into question the Maastricht process, some speakers stressed the incompatibility between Europe's current economic objectives and its employment goals. In their view, the cautious approach taken by Europe's leaders was doing more than any specific policy to depress the level of employment.

But if the economy is to be boosted, *what kind of growth* do we want? The NGOs recommended that growth should be directed towards job creation and the social economy, so as to achieve sustainable growth that would take account of the environment and the quality of life. The NGOs also stressed that gross domestic product (GDP) as a measure of growth was becoming 'more and more discredited' and called on Europe to be guided by the work of the UNDP[57] on 'human development'.

---

[57] United Nations Development Programme.

Chapter 6

More ambitious employment policies

Most speakers were in favour of taking action to promote employment and to combat exclusion and most proposals called for ambitious policies, which we will first of all present in outline before describing the three guiding themes.

6.1. THE BASIC PRINCIPLES

'Mainstreaming'

This buzzword, popular in European circles, refers to the key principle that social and employment considerations must be at the heart of the various policies and not just on the margins, with 'positive discrimination' in favour of disadvantaged groups. Action has been taken along these lines to ensure equal opportunities between men and women. Might it now be possible to build on this in more general terms to promote employment and combat exclusion?

Another key question relates to the *stage* at which mainstreaming should come into play: should it be afterwards (i.e. in an evaluation) or before, in the context of a genuine preventive policy? This preventive dimension, stressed by several participants, ties in with the earlier debate: should economic and financial criteria be the 'primary' criteria of the European Union? In other words, we come back to the problem of conceptions: should economic stability come first or should we give priority to synergy between the economy and society 'from the outset'? As long as we remain locked into a binary system of 'economy or society' (or rather economy → society), employment policies will only ever have a limited impact.

Partnership

This 'portmanteau word', used many times during the debate, was at the heart of the report produced by P. Townsend. It was principally the NGOs which spoke on this subject, calling for a greater role not only in the implementation but also in the drafting of policies. They would like to be consulted more systematically on these subjects by the Commission and by Parliament. They also ask that their role as employers be recognized and supported in the context of this social and mutually supportive economy, whose impact should be greater in the future. Their role should in particular be recognized by the new European Social Fund, which the NGOs fear will be used by the public authorities for their own benefit only.

The social partners saw their important role reaffirmed in the struggle against unemployment and exclusion. Firms have a duty to be 'citizens', that is to take responsibility vis-à-vis their workers in the context of a preventive policy on the organization of work (cf. Green Paper)[58] but also *vis-à-vis* their local environment, both social and ecological. Most participants took this line, except . . . the employers! Is this a pious hope? Could the European Union not negotiate with the major transnational firms (whose economic impact is much greater than that of countries) so that they fall into line with this kind of vision?

---

[58] Partnership for a new organisation of work – European Commission Green Paper, Luxembourg, EUR-OP, 1997, 18p. ISBN 9278186724.

The role of trade unions was also reaffirmed, but they are barely representative in many countries and have not succeeded, for the moment, in counterbalancing the globalization of firms.

As for the public authorities, and in particular governments, their role was seen as essential, not only as a welfare state combating social polarization, but also as leader of this partnership, which is increasingly failing to balance economy and society. It is up to governments to guarantee social stability, but they need to give more support to civil society (trade unions, NGOs, and especially unemployed people's associations), which has often been weakened by the steamroller of the economy.

Moving beyond welfare

The theme of participation and citizenship, which was the subject of another of the workshops, could not be overlooked in a debate on the future world of work, given that numerous unemployed people's associations were represented at the Forum.

All the participants insisted on the need to move beyond 'welfare' and to redirect employment and anti-exclusion policies. Priority should be given to supporting the various players and especially to encouraging involvement and creativity among the disadvantaged sections of the population. As the UK Secretary of State, Mr Blunkett, pointed out, it is people themselves who constitute the main asset, not only those who are in difficulties or who have potential which must be harnessed, but all of us, who must be proactive on behalf of the excluded. It is a responsibility which we have to ourselves in a democracy.

Mr Blunkett went on to explain that we must reject 'services for the poor' because these are 'poor services'. This ties in with the earlier discussion of 'workfare', which should not result in ghettos for the poor or in a new form of forced labour.

6.2. STIMULATING EMPLOYMENT

The various proposals put forward can be divided into three categories. The first category comprises those that aim to facilitate job creation, especially in new fields of activity. The second comprises proposals for better regulation of the labour market so as to reconcile flexibility and security. The third category includes those proposals that focus on mobilizing additional financial resources to create new room for manoeuvre.

Facilitating the creation of jobs and new sectors of activity

A certain consensus was reached on three complementary themes, even though there were differences in emphasis:

- *The development of the social/mutually supportive economy*, dealt with in detail by Professor Borzaga, would require specific support from the public authorities (status, making resources available to meet demand), allowing its full potential to be exploited despite the fact that demand is not easily defined. To enhance its credibility, this sector needs investment in high-quality services and closer links with the traditional economy. Although, as the trade-union representative stressed, the social economy is not *the* answer to unemployment (no-one spoke of it as a 'new source of employment') it is nevertheless the most important avenue for the creation of new sectors of activity and jobs.
- *The idea of assisting the creation of new companies, SMEs and micro-enterprises* received more support from the employers' representatives. It is part of their conception of flexibility, whose negative aspects are too often all we remember (as their spokesperson pointed out, it should be possible to set up a business without having to consult a legal expert!). As for SMEs, while they often call for tax or para-fiscal advantages – as they did

144

during this debate – their principal needs may in fact be for advisory, engineering or local community services so that they too can achieve their full potential. Emphasis was also placed on the inadequacy of the information available on SMEs/SMIs.

- *A more employment-friendly tax and para-fiscal tax system* was also advocated, with social security contributions no longer based solely on manpower and with specific advantages for certain job-creating sectors (e.g. personal services). However, tax advantages in respect of part-time work were more controversial.

Reconciling flexibility and security on the labour market

As explained above, consensus was more difficult to reach on this subject because of the approach taken by the employers, which advocated 'external' flexibility.

None the less, the employers' representative acknowledged the need to regulate new forms of employment, accepting some 'give and take' between such regulation and the dismantling of certain rigidities (annualization of working time, night work for women).[59]

In view of the rapid increase in part-time work (too often a second choice) one contributor put forward the idea of an overall reduction in working time. Although this path is currently being followed in France, it does not seem to be having much effect.

Scarcely any mention was made of the underground economy, seen as a dangerous competitor for the official economy rather than a possible source of new jobs. One way of combating the underground economy might be to individualize social rights, so as to avoid secondary rights, thus making it easier to work on the black market, but this would be an enormous task!

---

[59] A policy followed notably in the Netherlands (see article on the scientific literature, especially the contribution by Jacqueline O'Reilly and Claudia Spee).

With a view to helping the jobless become more active, the representative of ATD Quart Monde drew attention to the limits of unemployment benefit, which does not encourage a return to work or promote mutual support among the unemployed: it is a real poverty trap that the current systems are hollowing out beneath their feet.

Releasing new resources

As pointed out by the rapporteur P. Townsend, the resources available for the European Union's structural policies are far from insignificant: total expenditure over the period 1989–99 amounted to 6.5 per cent of the Community's annual GDP, which is not so different, in relative terms, from the amount of aid given fifty years ago under the Marshall Plan (4 per cent of Europe's GDP between 1948 and 1951). Some 30 per cent of assistance from the Structural Funds goes towards improving education and training systems and supporting employment policies.[60] It was unfortunately not possible, for lack of data, to discuss whether the Social Fund's share in the Structural Funds should be increased or even to think about another direction for this Fund, which so far has tended essentially to focus on improving people's employability, although – as was said more than once – that is not the problem. Above all, we need to find a solution to the lack of jobs.

As pointed out in the preliminary report, 70 per cent of assistance from the European Structural Funds is allocated to infrastructure and to supporting productive investment. But what kind of 'productive' investment are we talking about? We come back to our earlier point regarding the 'real' economy: should a massive *redeployment* to local initiatives and new service activities not be part of the agenda for the European Structural Funds?

---

[60] This is the European Social Fund, to which the NGOs wished to have greater access, whereas the Member States tended to 'appropriate' it for their own purposes.

Such a redeployment of expenditure was also suggested in connection with the budgets of the various Member States of the European Union. Given the limits laid down by the Treaty of Maastricht (limits whose appropriateness was contested by certain participants), should public expenditure not be restructured to make it employment-friendly? These concerns reflect the desire to move from passive policies to others which are more active, but still, unfortunately, formulated in terms of 'supporting access to employment' instead of moving in the direction of *creating new jobs*. In Florence in 1996, with these same considerations in mind, the heads of State and Government reached an agreement to restructure public expenditure in favour of investment in human capital, research, innovation and infrastructures in order, *inter alia,* to strengthen competitiveness. A positive step forward, but one geared to a competitive economy, which is not necessarily the most job-rich type of economy.

Given the limits inherent in this kind of redeployment approach, the question arises as to whether new types of financing should be found for job creation and the fight against exclusion. D. Meulders proposes introducing a tax on CO_2 emissions, with a view to ensuring sustainable development, or the famous 'Tobin tax'[61] on cross-border financial transactions, which would counteract the increasingly financial nature of the world economy and raise US\$150 billion each year at world level.

The answer to the first question (not discussed) depends on whether Europe is able to strike out alone: is its economic and political weight sufficient to lead the rest of the world, including the United States, in the direction of better international regulation? The second question relates to the difficulties of European political union: according to D. Meulders, the unanimity rule

---

[61] James Tobin, winner of the Nobel Prize for Economics, invented the idea of a tax on capital movements in the 1970s. He proposed introducing a tax at a low rate (0.1 per cent or even 0.01 per cent) on each financial transaction so as to penalize capital movements.

will have to be abolished if this kind of tax is to have a chance of being approved.

According to the European Social Forum and its workshop on work, the key challenge for European employment policy is to 'keep hold of both ends of the chain': *action involving people* and *action involving structures*, instead of contenting itself with a mediocre 'between the two' approach, which does not fundamentally solve the problems.

On the one hand, policies need to be anchored in human dignity: men and women need to be valued as the main resource in the economy, but must not be considered exclusively in that light. This requirement forms the basis for rejecting everything that resembles forced labour or the relentless pursuit of economism and precarious employment situations where the individual has to bow to the bidding of his masters. Hence the need to be anchored in the local culture and mentality but also (so as to rediscover a little common sense and to reject the excesses of economism) to return to the reality of poverty, to look it in the face and to listen to what its victims have to say.

On the other hand, anchoring policies in the individual and then contenting ourselves with that could have perverse consequences. We might impose on the excluded a kind of 'order to integrate', developing all sorts of programmes to assist and train them, forcing them to 'go round in circles' in a 'process of integration'.[62] This does not give them access to genuine occupational integration, for the biggest problem remains the insufficient number of jobs.

It is therefore essential to go back to the source of the problem by dealing with structures and with an economic system that does not create enough jobs, in particular for disadvantaged groups. More decisive support is needed for local development, SMEs, the social economy and, more generally, whatever will

---

[62] Robert Castel, *Les métamorphoses de la question sociale*, Fayard 1995.

generate work – without increasing poverty. This clearly requires us to counteract an international economic system that is not moving in this direction, and, more fundamentally, to challenge the dominant economic ideas.

Civil society is thus calling on the European Union to go one step further: Europe must not simply try to keep on top of globalization, but should seek to promote a model of civilization which fits its culture and an international economic system which gives the individual all the space he deserves.

Conclusions

The future of work: an unending and impossible debate in Europe? This could be the conclusion naturally reached by anyone reading the texts collected together in this publication.

Work, like democracy, liberty or solidarity, is a recurrent subject of debate in Europe; it is therefore not surprising that the very mention of its disappearance and the questions as to what it will become lend themselves more to an exchange of controversial remarks than to the construction of thorough arguments and realistic proposals.

The discussion launched within the Commission had no other purpose than to fill these gaps. Looked at from this point of view, the message is rather more encouraging: the preceding chapters demonstrate clearly the Commission's capacity to add to national debates and to transcend sectoral divisions, although they also expose the difficulty Europeans have with facing up to their future and their reluctance to contemplate substantial reforms to the current system.

Such an abrupt conclusion, however, would not do justice to the wealth of lessons that the Commission departments were able to draw from the exercise. Among them, four deserve to be described in detail:

- *First,* national and regional diversity merely adds subtlety to the debate on what is essentially a common European concern. The literature reviews and the debate at the Social Forum confirm the instinctive feeling that the changing nature of work and the concerns which this provokes – not to mention the anxieties – go beyond national and cultural specifics. Historically, Europe has always been a theatre for intense exchanges of ideas. It is even more so now that the social dimension of European integration is developing and acquiring political stature. But the debate becomes fiercer and wider when changes deeply shake the foundations of social organization. It is not surprising, therefore, that discussions are fiercest in Sweden, Germany and France, where the industrial model has been perfected many times and where governments traditionally base their actions on theoretical concepts. On the other hand, there is more of a wait-and-see attitude in countries where policy is a more pragmatic exercise (in the United Kingdom or the Netherlands) or where the 'curse' of work remains external to the functioning of society (as in the Mediterranean countries).

- *Second,* no clear path of action emerges from the discussions of the theoreticians and experts.

They merely put us on our guard as to the uncertain future of work. Researchers, whether from Europe or America, are more inclined to discuss diagnoses and causes than to devise any real solutions. But can we blame them? Is that not what political leaders are meant to do? Regrettably, the academics do not provide us with enough evidence to enable us to take decisions with full knowledge of the facts. Perhaps they have not given up the dream of one day finding *the* cause of all our ills and thus providing *the* miracle solution...

None the less, when theory (the three literature reviews) is compared with practice (the analysis of occupational behaviour in local initiatives and the Social Forum debate), the impression arises that some phenomena are overvalued. Solutions such as work-sharing, teleworking, lifelong learning, etc. lack visibility and/or substance and have not been implemented on a large scale.

The end of work seems more of a slogan than a reality. Its advocates tend to underestimate the values of the post-industrial society that is emerging, establishing itself not in opposition to industrial society, but on the rubble of that society and of the consumer society. In other words, Europeans are more concerned with ecology, organic produce and alternative medicine, but are reluctant to give up private cars, the telephone, or even the comfort provided by nuclear-generated electricity. Likewise, they aspire to greater individual autonomy and personal development but remain strongly attached to all the social redistribution mechanisms inherited from the postwar period.

- *Third,* choosing to reform the social model step by step is probably equivalent to abandoning any reform.

It is impressive to see how far the trade unions, professional organizations and associations have come in ten years. Their transformation shows us how quickly society has cast off – easily or painfully, depending on the circumstances – the burdens of the industrial model. For all that, the whole institutional mechanism is not showing any signs of major change, which demonstrates the inherent contradiction: progressive reform is impossible because of the stable and balanced nature of the model.

This is surely a challenge to those who, while they believe in the need to reform the European social model, are equally strongly opposed to its disappearance. We have a vague feeling that the current debate opens up new prospects but that, for lack of broad popular support, we will have to abandon these hopes for some decades at best, and indefinitely at worst. Taking an optimistic view, we can be confident that mentalities will evolve, but that it will take a generation or so and we will just have to wait twenty or thirty years. But, on a pessimistic view, we have to admit that the question 'Will there be a job for everyone tomorrow?' will come to seem ridiculous once the demographic decline in the developed countries forces us to recruit labour from other parts of the world.

- *Fourth,* the difficult emergence of a democratic vision attached to the new reality of work constitutes a major obstacle for Europe.

153

In wondering what the future of work will be and what its place in society is, we quickly come to challenge the presuppositions on which policy commitments and some rules of the democratic game are based. This debate updates the dividing lines between political parties, which go beyond the traditional divisions between left and right. Among the three identifiable positions, we of course find the classic distinction between those who believe in liberty above all and those who favour cohesion and equality. But there is also a third position, now in the process of being formulated. It finds expression through certain local initiatives and the action of some representatives of associations, trade unions and employer organizations, but is has not yet been translated into political action. The advocates of this third way are well aware that in seeking alliances, their ideas could be compromised or simply obscured. As a result, they take refuge in theory, seeming like prophets of a distant utopia. None the less, we feel that they could significantly change the terms of the social and political debate if they were to reach maturity.

So we find ourselves gradually being drawn into another debate but that debate is off limits: it extends well beyond the Commission's area of responsibility and beyond the scope of this discussion. But scaling down our ambitions does not mean there is nothing to be done: we just have to take one by one the numerous avenues outlined in the three literature reviews and the Social Forum discussion. They suggest that if the European Union is to remain the guarantor of social cohesion, it can (and must) take two courses of action. It has:

– first, to provide security, paying greater attention to change to ensure that any progress in the areas of flexibility and competitiveness is not made at the expense of the most disadvantaged or to the detriment of the less fortunate;

– second, to inspire, support and provide impetus for certain lifestyle and work trends. It involves endeavouring to outstrip economically induced changes by backing certain groups of the population or making deliberate breaks to re-establish a new continuity, either at territorial level or in the lives of individuals.

Such a conclusion may seem minor by comparison with the issues debated. Yet it would be a mistake to think that the current practice of the Commission and the other European institutions leads us automatically in that direction. Both the first and second courses of action call for important decisions and difficult choices. In any event, they can only be pursued with the support of partners from the world of work and civil society . . . and perhaps one day the political world.

The Forward Studies Unit

The Forward Studies Unit[63] was set up in 1989 as a department of the European Commission reporting direct to the President.

It consists of a multicultural, multidisciplinary team of some 15 staff who are responsible for monitoring the forward march of European integration while identifying structural trends and long-term prospects.

The Commission decision in setting the Unit up[64] gave it three tasks:

- to monitor and evaluate European integration to 1992 and beyond;
- to establish permanent relations with national bodies involved in forecasting;
- to work in specific briefs.

The Forward Studies Unit has, to date, produced wide-ranging reports on new issues which, as a result, have frequently found their way into the mainstream of the Commission's work, developing a house style which applies a research method designed to bring out the diversity of Europe (Shaping Factors, Shaping Actors), developing an all-round and/or long-term view which makes it easier to secure consensus above and beyond particular national interests, keeping a watching brief on and an ear open to movement in Europe's societies by setting up links with

---

[63] European Commisison, Forward Studies Unit, ARCH-25, Rue de la Loi 200, B-1049 Brussels, tel. + 32-2-295-6735, fax +32-2-295-2305, Internet http://europa.eu.int

[64] Minutes of the 955th meeting of the European Commission, 8 March 1989.

research and forward studies institutions, and holding regular seminars on specific themes which are attended by prominent figures from the arts, the cultural sphere and universities and representatives of civil society, together with the President or a Member of the European Commission.

The futurological function has gradually developed outside the Unit, within several of the Commission's Directorates-General which are keen to adopt a strategic approach. The Unit serves as a point where all the various future-oriented think tanks inside the Commission can meet.

For some years now, the need for a forecasting function having grown as the work of the European Union has become wider and more complex, the work programme for the Forward Studies Unit has been updated each year so that it can be reoriented to meet specific needs and towards maximum cooperation with all the Commission departments concerned.

Information about the Unit's current work is put out in the quarterly *Lettre des Carrefours* and on an Internet site.

OTHER TITLES PUBLISHED IN THIS SERIES

Democracy and the Information Society in Europe
The New Economics of Sustainable Development
The Future of North-South Relations
Shaping Actors, Shaping Factors in Russia's Future
Towards a More Coherent Economic Global Order
The Mediterranean Society – A Challenge for Islam, Judaism and Christianity